OLDHAM

&

its people

Freda Millett

OLDHAM
Leisure Services

Published by Oldham Arts and Heritage Publications, 1994.
Oldham Leisure Services,
Civic Centre, West Street, Oldham OL1 1XJ.

© Freda Millett 1994

ISBN 0 902809 31 8

Reprinted 1995

Designed by Oldham Leisure Services
Typesetting by Mike Johnson Typesetting
Printing by Snape Printers Ltd.

*Cover photograph: Members of the Oldham Borough police and
fire service Athletic and Recreation society on a day out at
Hardcastle Crags in 1933. Matty Lalley – a well known Oldham
policeman and his family are on the right of the photograph, third row up.*

Contents

Photographs
This page: Royal visit to Oldham, 1954.
Opposite page, top: Mill girls in new overalls for the Queen's visit.
below: Chronicle Employees Christmas Party, c1958.

'Waiting for Dad'
outside Red Lion in Lees

Day Trip
to Alexandra Park

Acknowledgements

I would like to pay tribute to the generosity of the Oldham people who have loaned their precious photographs for inclusion in this publication. Not all the photographs contributed have found a place in the book but I can assure readers that all photos have been copied and are now a valued part of Oldham Local Studies Library archives. Keith Andrew, Otto Adler, Eileen Batley, Mrs. Billington, Ken Blair, Olga Bradbury, Mary Beels, Joan Brennan, Sybil Buck, H & O. Butterworth, Albert Charlesworth, Sheila Collier, Terence Conn, Barry Cook, Ron Crawford, Harvey Crossland, Jack Crossley, Sybil Curley, Joe Dawson, Brian Dixon, Irene Dickinson, Ken Foulston, John & May Fawley, Gladys Farrow, Betty & Paul Foden, Arthur Force, Vera Gillespie, Derek & Annie Geary, Mrs. Gilligan, Mildred Hamer, Judith Haughton, Annice Hawley, Pat Heap, Rosemary Hester, Joyce Hibbert, Harry Hirst, Nora Hirst, Marcus Holloway, Maurice Holloway, David Hotton, Vera Hyatt, Derek Hyde, Mr. & Mrs. W. Ireland, Florence Jacks, Mr. & Mrs. F. Jackson, Amy Kent, Margaret Kennedy, Mabaswir Khan, Jack Kirkbride, Eva Kime, Oleksander Korolczuk, John Laine, Evelyn Lees, Roy Lees, Reg Lees, Joan Lawton, Eddie Lumley, Miss Laister, Alan Leach, C. Marshall, Norma Mottley, Ralph & Dorothy Mellor, Chadwick Middleton, David McKenzie, Sonia Mather, Mr. & Mrs. Kahil Mir, Nadia & Stefan Moroz, Vishnu Mohandas, George Nutter, Edith & Jack Parsons, Joyce Plant, John Pellowe, Audrey Pickerill, Elaine & Ivan Padmore, Albert Ramsden, Margaret Riley, Alexandra Rymaszewski, Sheila Senior, Irene Scragg, Bharat Sisodia, Martin & Jurica Smith, Doreen Smith, Lucy Slater, Ivy Standing, Norman Stoller, Eric Sykes, Elsie Taylor, Roland & Marjorie Taylor, Moreen Walkden, Kenneth Ward, Lesley & Alan Webb, Marjorie Wood, Edith & Sam Wild, Marjorie & Alan Wolstencroft, Margaret Wilson, Hilda Williams, Madelaine Yavorsky.

Special gratitude is offered to the Oldham Chronicle and their helpful staff who always respond to my obscure requests for help and advice with interest and enthusiasm.

Coronation
Celebrations
John Booth Street

Slater Street
Children 1930's

Kenneth and Harry
Hirst on holiday

Boy's Brigade
on parade in
Lees – before
library built

Oldham Centenary.
Marie Nally, Oldham Cotton Queen on right

Foreword

Clearly, any book which is made up of people's
memories cannot be true for everyone – some things
will be good to remember and many will be hard to
forget ... even when there exists a sweet,
philosophical resignation which eases the sadness.
In an age when conservationists are trying to
preserve our old buildings, our beautiful landscapes
and our wild creatures, thankfully, making us all
more aware of these important issues, it is hard to
imagine that once upon a time other happenings
had more urgency .....

Above: Harry and Marion Hirsts' wedding c1922. Kenneth Hirst,
former Editor of the Oldham Chronicle as pageboy.
Top: Mayor and Mayoress of Oldham (Alderman and Mrs Bardsley) 1933.
'Lamb' holiday fund provided a trip to Hoylake for children in their
last year at school who had never visited the seaside.

Introduction

This is a story about real people of Oldham in their own words – those – having gone to pastures new, denying the call of the moors and those who have stayed, hugging their handcuffs to their hearts, perhaps dreaming of future release.

It would be straining the imagination of the most dedicated poet to call Oldham a pretty place. It has never been. It has no pine woods, few streets lined with trees and in appearance is often unendearing .. but here I belong and I write of it with affection. It is possible to take a bus ride or even a twenty minute walk and find profound silence and views so hypnotic that driving has to be negotiated carefully. Oldham people like to remind themselves that the town was once one of the most important industrial areas in England and evidence of the extraordinary genius of local inventors, builders and architects is present in the majestic mills still defiantly dominating the landscape.

As a child I knew the centre of Oldham only through the occasional shopping trip. Living barely a stones throw away I, like most other children, created an enclosed world which was seldom strayed from – until the teenage years when the bright lights and the big band sounds beckoned. . . . .

To compile this publication, I have recorded the memories of around sixty people – some individually and others as a group. The period covered is the 1920s to the 1960s.

Sometimes it has only been possible to pick out fragments from the colourful tapestry of these years and I hope the end product provides an intriguing contrast with todays standard of community life.

A LAND FIT FOR HEROES

The 'roaring twenties' – as they became known – did not start roaring right away. Indeed, for huge numbers of the poor, they never roared at all.

The end of the 1914-1918 war had brought irrevocable changes for women – the most important one being the right to vote. This new and much fought for privilege was reflected in their dress – the previous soberness having been blown to bits on the French battlefields.

'I remember coming downstairs, ready to go out – in this frock, it was just above the knee and skimpy, the material had no bant in it. On me, it wasn't very revealing, because I had no bosom then. I think it was the only time in my life that I have been in fashion. I'd had my hair bobbed and when my father saw me, he was aghast, "What's the world coming to?" he said, "I don't think the vote will do these girls any good, or the country for that matter, thank God, she can't vote for a few years yet!". What he didn't realise was that I didn't give a damn about voting, 30 years old seemed a long time away, I just wanted a good time, I wasn't interested in politics.'

'So many lives were lost and so many young men never returned home again after the first world war. These women are either widowed or unmarried as a result of that war. They all worked together at a holiday home in Wales.'

Visit of the Prince of Wales to Oldham in the1920s

Everyone wanted peace at any price, they were tired of war, tired of sadness and there was a tendency to look back to pre-war prosperity. Young men who had narrowly escaped death in the trenches were returning to their loved ones with the memory of burying their comrades in Flanders behind them. The huge numbers returning to civilian life led to widespread unemployment and a housing shortage.

'When my father came home after the war, my mother and her two sisters had died in the flu epidemic and my sister and me had been put in the workhouse. I was four years old and my sister a couple of years older. My mother had been buried as a pauper. This is something I realised as I grew older. It was because my father was at war and unable to see to anything – the house was only rented anyway. I can remember it now – they put her on a handcart, it was flat with lamps at each corner. He came to the workhouse and got us out, but we had no home, so he took us to live at my Aunty Kitty's on Drury Lane – I slept with my Aunty Kitty and Uncle Ernie, three in a bed and my sister slept in the back room with my Uncle Albert – my father was in lodgings as well because he had no home to go back to. We were in two more lodgings after this with my father – one of them where the woman was always drunk and used to pawn our clothes. By the time I was 10 years old we had happy lodgings at last at 899 Hollins Road, it was the best home we ever had, but the war had obviously wrecked my Dad's life.'

Twenty years later the two sisters, Mary, Annie and Mary's son William with Mrs. Breakell of 899 Hollins Road

Above Top: These men have just finished building the power station on Broadway after the First World War and are having a break.
On the back of the photograph it says 'God bless them all'.

Above: Coal picking

The previous booming economy of Oldham whose population had grown at a tremendous pace had come to an abrupt end and the long period of buoyant self confidence that had been achieved with the cotton industry suddenly floundered. Although the 20s was a revolutionary time with the wireless, cinema, cars and the thrill of the first woman to take a seat in Parliament, it was also a decade of hidden misery and only occasional surface gaiety. In Oldham, men would stand at street corners in groups and the phrase eloquently quoted by Lloyd George 'a country fit for heroes to live in,' sounded like a joke.

'My Aunty Bertha must have never given in, now that I'm older I can see it clearly. We were all living there at the time. I don't know why, must have been because my father had no work, because when I was coming home from school he would be sat on the wall at the bottom of the street with a lot of other fellas. They must all have been out of work. Everybody used their back doors then and

my Aunty Bertha would be stood at the sink – sleeves rolled up and the fattest arms that you have every seen and she'd be singing "Let the great big world keep turning". My Uncle Jim would say "for Christ sake, can't someone shut that woman up".'

The great expectations after the war ended were shattered in a massive economic recession and the men who returned had still to face the bitterness of the General Strike in 1926.

The response to the strike call was overwhelming. In spite of the Government arguing that the strike was unconstitutional, the strikers acted unselfishly to support the miner's claim to a living wage. Oldham was hit badly, as coal, which underlies much of the town, was vital to the growth of local industry. Some of the mills were located near to the collieries and depended on coal for power.

The mine owners claimed that wages should be cut, demanding a $13\frac{1}{2}$ per cent reduction in miner's pay. Stanley Baldwin who was the Prime Minister stated that not only miners but also all other workers would have to accept wage reductions. In Oldham there were few demonstrations, but eventually the seriousness of the strike struck home and because most of the houses in the town had coal fires, supplies ran out.

'My mother couldn't go and dig for coal on the Edge, because our Billy was only a wee baby, but as soon as we came home from school we had to go. We took the tin bath, well, you can imagine, it took a lot of filling and people had got their own little spots to dig, they must have thought we had big ideas when they saw us with this great huge bath, it went on for weeks!'

Left: Oldham Group from the
Independent Labour
party rooms, day out.
Below: Clarion Clubhouse,
Greenfield Front Row: Sam Firth,
Eddie Whyatt, Ethel Starkey,
Ernest Whyatt, Willie Whyatt
and Mrs. Firth. 1920's

'Platts had partly closed down and with others I went on Oldham Edge digging for coal from old workings. Knowing I could drive, Platts recalled me and asked if I was prepared to drive one of their lorries carrying goods between the Hartford new works and the old works. I enthusiastically agreed, but had some doubts when they gave me the handle of a pick-axe to protect myself in the event of an attack by pickets, however, no such event occurred.'

The general strike involving most industries lasted for nine days but nearly forty-five thousand railwaymen all over Britain didn't return to work for another five months. The miner's slogan 'Not a minute on the day, not a penny off the pay', fell on deaf ears as after seven months of continued unemployment their spirit was broken and the miners, for their families' sake, returned to work, accepting a reduced wage.

'When I signed on at the employment exchange (my *only* experience in spite of being brought up in a depressed area), it will always stay in my memory, because of what seemed to me to be an attack on personal dignity. There was a large notice behind the clerk which said "If you have no work, do not wait for the clerk to ask – say – no work". I thought it was appalling that the applicant was denied the courtesy of a short question from the clerk, which with the answer would have been an exchange of civilities between two fellow humans. I flatly refused to conform and always stood in front of the counter silent until the clerk irritably asked the question. I don't suppose my attitude did any good; the clerk probably thought I was too stupid to know what was expected of me.'

'The Independent Labour Party was created in Oldham after the General Strike, they met in rooms over Bottom of the Moor Stores, it was a Co-op building. We held whist drives and dances on Saturday nights. The League of Youth was formed and we would go out in a large group on Sundays, some of our discussions would become quite heated. There was a meeting every Sunday night outside Alexandra Park gates, which was a place for political meetings. All kinds of people came to speak – we got a good crowd. The Rev. Gordon Lang was MP for Oldham in the late 20s for the Independent Labour Party – he put up against the original Labour party. We used to sing, "Vote, Vote, Vote for Lang and Wilson!" . . . '

Below: Digging for coal in Oldham during the 1920 Miners' Strike

In 1921, the boxing match between Dempsey and Carpentier was the first thing to be broadcast and people bought radio sets to hear the commentary on the fight. It was the World Heavyweight Championship. These radios needed accummulators, which were lead acid batteries in glass containers which could be recharged at the corner shop for a few pennies. This method was terribly inconvenient and the batteries unreliable.

'I was sent to the shop carrying the accumulator, which was damned heavy and all kids were used to *running* errands, but you couldn't run with one of these, you had visions of dropping it and all this acid burning your socks and your legs. I don't know if it would, but the thought of it was enough, it was very thick glass mind you'.

In April of 1923 the new stadium at Wembley was first used for the Cup Final. The teams were West Ham and Bolton Wanderers. Huge crowds surged to the ground, many from the North and because of the chaos the game started much later than advertised. The barriers were broken down and the turnstiles refused to cope with the demands.

'I was 16 – it was a bit frightening I can tell you, but the excitement of being there overcame that, I went with my father and two others he worked with. There was a special train laid on from Manchester.'

At the end of the decade radio sets had improved immensely from a simple 'crystal set' with a long, outside aerial and a pair of earphones, to a receiver which was capable of picking up radio signals over long distances.

'When we got the radio, that day I couldn't wait to get home from school. I brought about six kids home with me, but my mother wouldn't touch it, she was scared of it – this is 1933 mind – when I think today, little children of four years can put a video on! We had to wait until my father came home, my mother gave all my friends a jam butty and sent them packing.'

Wembley 1923

A JOB FOR LIFE

Comptometer table in the Check Office at Oldham Industrial Co-op Society. The dividend was calculated on these machines.

My Grandma took me to sit this exam at the Co-op. We all sat round an enormous table, in which I realised years later was the committee room and there were three men – the Manager, Mr Walker, the Secretary, Mr Boden and the Chairman, who I think was John Friend. Someone said "You may begin" and we had to do some arithmetic, write an application, read a passage from a book and answer some questions on it.

A few days later a letter came to say I'd got the job. My Gran was so thrilled, herself having lived through the hungry thirties – she said it was a 'job for life' – which I didn't find very inspiring, and she was everywhere, telling everyone.'

'The Check Office at the Co-op Society was like one big family, everybody knew everything about everybody. They shared happiness and sadness. I remember a lot of singing and at divi' time when we were sorting and adding, everything was geared to getting the divi' out on time – dividend couldn't be late – too many people depended on it.'

'I had always been interested in films and Mum knew the chap who worked at the King's cinema, so she had a word with him. People used that expression "I'll have a word with him" a lot then . Anyway, I started at the Kings cinema as a trainee projectionist.' 'The King's at that time was owned by R.H. Coops' – who were coffin-makers and undertakers. They had their place next door to the Mess House and they had a fleet of 1935 Daimlers in a huge garage at the top of Fairbottom Street. They also used one part of this building as stables where they kept their team of black horses. Right up to the early 1950s, if people wanted that kind of funeral, they could be accommodated. '

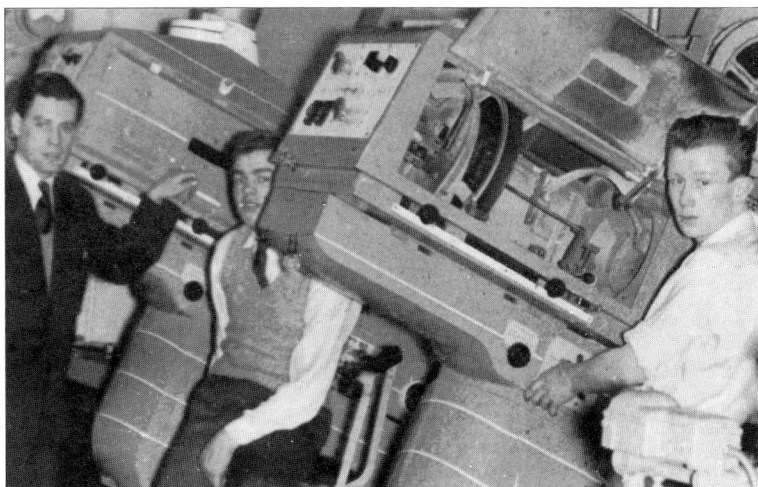

'I eventually left the King's to go to the Gaumont as co-chief projectionist. Dimmers and sound system used at the Gaumont cinema in the 1950s made it look like the interior of a space rocket.'

Mill girls at Lilac Mill, Shaw

People starting work in the 20s and 30s were often employed in jobs far below their intelligence and ability and although educational opportunities were theoretically much better than they had been fifty or a hundred years earlier, had they been born a generation later a proportion of them at least would have had higher aspirations. These young people had to earn their living during a period of huge and demoralising unemployment.

'I remember vividly my father's chest trouble, brought on by breathing the cotton dust in the mill. It got worse and worse, until we all dreaded his coming home from work. He would stagger through the door and grasp the nearest solid support, resting until he could finally get across the room and sink into a chair, gasping for breath. Later he would eat some food and go to bed to recuperate ready for the renewed struggle next day. I actually witnessed this day after day. Why did he battle on like this? Simply because the idea of not working and being dependent on sick pay, appalled him and not only for the great reduction in income. My two elder brothers tramped across the Pennines into Yorkshire because they heard a rumour of work there. When they found none, they walked back and mended their boots, worn down by the long hike.'

Peter and Alf – beam setters at Regent Mill, Failsworth 1937. Mill ghost on right?

'We bought this shop in 1947 and everyone thought we were out of our minds – it was so run-down, but that was the only way we could have afforded it. I was getting a bit fed-up – just looking after babies and I really wanted a little job – so I thought this was a good idea, because I didn't have to leave them. Slowly, but surely we built the stock up and eventually it became a typical corner shop which sold almost everything. It was on the corner of Boundary Park Road, right next door to the Latics and all the footballers came in . . . George Hardwick I remember and many more. We stayed in it for fourteen years and made lots of friends. The photograph (left) is of my two children, Margaret and Clive.'

Bank Top Mill, Lees during the war: Audrey Boden, Joyce Kenworthy, Jean Pass, Alice Chorlton.

'I started work at a sewing place down Hollinwood – I detest sewing but I don't think they knew what to put me to. I think they could tell at home I was very unhappy. However, Dunkerley's Woodend Mill was near home and I had always been friendly with their daughter Margaret who was in my class at Knolls Lane – so my dad asked John Dunkerley to fix me up – which he did. During the war, a lot of the mills couldn't get cotton across to England, so Woodend Mill closed down. I had to go to the Employment Exchange – they wanted to send me to Chorley to an underground munitions works. I'd heard about the place – someone told me the stuff they used, made you go yellow. I told them I didn't want to go there and my mother was dependent on my money – which she was in a way, because I had two little sisters. I suppose they could have insisted,but they didn't, so I was lucky I suppose. I eventually got a job on my own at the Bank Top Mill here in Lees.'

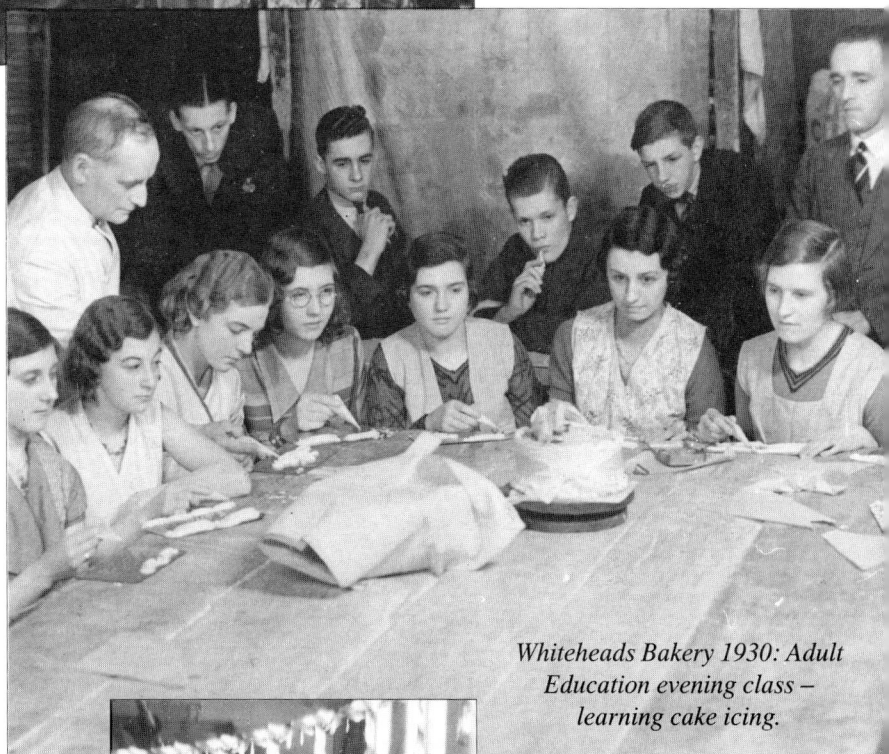

Whiteheads Bakery 1930: Adult Education evening class – learning cake icing.

'I'll tell you why many of us were shoved into jobs we perhaps didn't desire. For some people in the 20s in Oldham – after the First World War – life was very hard, especially if they hadn't got a house of their own. We all lived at my Grandma's and at the back of her house on Bow Street was the tripe shop, and the gas mantle shop was at the front of that and underneath they had cattle.

They killed the cattle further up and when they emptied the vats, they just rolled them down the back and it made a terrible smell. My father just went out one day with his best suit on – went and collected his wage and never returned. We've never seen him since. He left my mother with three little children and I had to go to work in the gas-mantle works. Circumstances decided a lot of things.'

Regent Mill, during the 1937 Coronation

Ramsden's Pork Butchers, Yorkshire Street, 1929. Fred Ramsden, second from left – front row.

Harry and Tom Hyde in front of Hyde's stall in the Victoria Market c1940s
'There was a great deal of competition between Pollards and ourselves. We had our
suppliers from Manchester – Abel Heywoods, and my father and Tom used to go down
to Clegg St. Station every morning – in time for the market opening. In the course of
time there was an agreement between Pollards and ourselves and they suggested that if
we bought from them, (they were wholesalers) they would quit selling in the market.'

Above: Wolfenden's gown shop, George St. 1949. Winners of Centenary window-dressing competition

Below: 'The foreman at Pellowes' was Granville Bradley and he used to teach us at night school, at the Technical College on Ascroft Street. It meant you couldn't peg off. This photograph shows us all visiting the old brick works at Booth Hill, about 1936.'

Left: Pellowes', Chamber Road c 1930

'I started at Pellowes' in 1933 as an apprentice joiner. Lewis Pellowe was a wonderful fellow to work for. He never asked a man to do a job he couldn't do himself. I've seen when we have had to make a couple of large windows and it could be about 3.30 p.m. - 4 o'clock. He's got the cutting list out – we've got going, all the preparing etc. and he had gone and brought back fish and chips because we would be late for our tea. When we had all gone home, he would paint the frames ready for morning. Lewis didn't differentiate between his son and his employees. John had to start at the bottom like anyone else. I've seen him as black as the ten of spades many times.'

'I didn't put much effort into my school work, I admit, but as far as getting a job was concerned, it was an understood thing that I would go into the family business, I really had no choice, not many young people did then. For the first three months the most important job I had was brewing up for everyone and then I was put onto a sanding machine, all the menial tasks actually. Then after a year I just about got a tool put into my hand. I was going to night school three nights a week for joinery. Pellowes' at that time had no transport, everything had to be delivered by handcart – eventually they got a van – but only the foreman could drive it. If you asked for overtime on Saturday morning, you got the tippler – toilet jobs – going round to the houses where the toilet wasn't turning over, it was a horrible job.'

The chimney on the right was due to be demolished at 6pm on the 2nd October 1930 but it collapsed unexpectedly just before at 5.05pm. On the left Pellowe & Sons, Hamilton and Jacks, are just seen – and the old Chamber Road Baptist.

Woolworths

*Paul Foden and his son,
John,*

William T. Grundy, pawnbroker

'Do you know then, you could go out in the morning and get a job and if you didn't like it, you could go out in the afternoon and get another. I went to work at Woolworths, a few of us went there from the Parish Church School – it was varied and interesting. I was put on the electrical ware counter and because of the complex collection of equipment, I learned quite a lot. Of course – some of it was fun and everyone was very friendly – we all knew each other. I remember a lady coming in one day for some flex, because she wanted the wireless moving – it was near the kitchen door and she wanted to move it into the recess at the side of the fireplace and I was trying to find out how much flex she would need so I said "Now where is your wireless?" and she said "It's over near the kitchen door"' and I asked "How far do you want to take it?" and she replied 'Hollinwood'.'

'When Geoffrey came out of the army – we decided we would start a little shop with his gratuity. We rented a shop from Oldham Brewery for 10/– a week. It was next to the Boltmakers Rest on the corner of Horsedge Street and Rock Street and it was an eye-opener.

'Oldham was like foreign parts, I only came from Audenshaw, but I'd never heard anything like the Oldham accent at the time. "Hasn't getten a packet of fags?" and "Just cobbed it down't ginnel", were like another language. People didn't travel to another town, unless they had relatives there. '

'The only time we sold toilet soap was Oldham Wakes, the shop didn't keep us – we kept the shop! I got a job at the Health Department next to the Town Hall and on Friday lunchtime I used to run home with my wages to pay the cigarette bill.

We made 10 per cent on sales so we hoped to take £100 a week, but there was no chance. People spent on average £2 odd a week with us and we had a tick book on the counter. We only survived because it was a food shop and at least we could eat. Geoff decided he would go and collect some debts, because we were getting desperate. One house he went to, the child who opened the door shouted "Mam, there's a man here for yer", the answer came "send him upstairs!".

Someone came in the shop, and said "Mrs Berry's not back!" by 6pm nobody had seen her. She was rather a strange old lady who would set off with a bag on each arm to the town, never seemed to buy anything – then came back with the same two bags. However this day – they came for Geoff. They looked through the window and somebody said "I think she's dead!". Geoff sent for the Police and they decided to break down her door – by this time there was a large queue forming for her house .. when she suddenly walked around the corner, quite oblivious to all the drama– walked into the house and banged the door!'

'I left school in 1924, when I was thirteen and went to work for a pawnbroker. I started at 6am until various times at night, depending on how busy we were. I got 10/– a week which wasn't bad pay then, but I must have worked at least 60 hours for that. It was an active trade and average pledges taken daily would be 200 to 300, which included suits, coats, shoes, boots, bundles of washing and clothing and jewellery. We had one particularly good customer who was a publican – he sent a diamond ring to be pledged every Monday for £10 to £25 and he would then lend the money out to his own customers with interest. It was good business also for the pawnbroker. Even false teeth and bicycles were pledged and my first bicycle was bought this way, after it had been forfeited after twelve months and seven days.'

*Left: Higher House,
Royton 1947. One of
the first Mill Nurseries*

*Above: Firbank homes.
1949. Miss Wilbraham
centre (Matron)*

'On the Saturday before the Whit-walks I have worked until one in the morning, serving people with Whitsuntide clothes they had pledged as much as 12 months previously. The tram stopped outside our shop from Royton and Rochdale and people going 'up town' would often leave something with us for a few bob and if they didn't spend their money they'd recover it. I looked at it this way, the rest of my family worked in the mill and I think my job gave me more variety.'

'I went to work in Hudsons in Oldham in 1937. The hours were 9am-8pm Monday-Friday and 9am-9pm Saturday. The wage was 6/– a week with a 2/– a year rise. My mother had to buy me a black dress and black stockings. I worked there until the war came – I was happy there, but I objected that I couldn't go to nightschool which started at 7pm. I fancied going into the Land Army – but when I got the form my Mum and Dad wouldn't sign it – so I was called up to go on munitions or the buses. My sister was on the buses during the war and the hours were awful – she was up at 4am and some evenings, on late shift, she didn't finish until nearly midnight . . . so I went on munitions and absolutely hated it. I was sat down all day – I was a spot welder at the Cape Mill and I was there five years – what an awful time! . . but it was during these years that I thought about going nursing. I had told my Mum – but she didn't want me to go away and if she had agreed, I would have been released from munitions. For a short time after the war I went into a cotton mill – cheese winding, because I didn't want to go back into shop work and I did just 5 months there.

I started off on a completely new career as a Nursery Nurse at Firbank Nursery. I never thought of these children as being neglected perhaps because we all loved them. We were never told any of the reasons why they were there. We only had the babies of course – there were homes in the grounds where the older children were, but we didn't have any involvement with them'.

Wages were low, salaries also. Discipline was rigid and often autocratic. It was accepted not to object too strongly or obviously to this situation because the labour market was well stocked and an employer would have no difficulty filling a vacancy. There were good and bad employers, the good ones have to be measured by the yardstick of their age and there is no doubt that the people who worked for them realised how fortunate they were and the pride in doing a job well became a basic human need and pleasure.

*On the Drill Hall roof.
Clifford Schofield in
centre, working for
Charlie Airey plumbers
1940's.*

Tate Street Nursery 1953. Sister with 'tweenies'

Eric Sykes and Hattie Jacques in Oldham Carnival

'When I came here in the winter of '47 – one of the worst winters on record, I had holes in my shoes and was suffering from malnutrition and was knocking at death's door (with a feather duster, mind you). I went to Oldham Rep. and I went for an audition and didn't want to go into straight acting, but I said "Don't say you'll let me know then as soon as I've closed that door, you'll forget." I thought that would happen actually, but the following Tuesday I got a telegram, I was at Oldham Rep. for six months, I worked one week in three and I got £3 a week, but I loved every minute of it and would have done it for nothing.

'I formed a dance band called the "Blue Sparks" and at one do we were so bad, we were fed off after the first number. We thought we would start with a Paul Jones and they started waltzing and the fellow who organised it came to the front of the stage and said "What are your expenses?" I said, "Have you got a back door?" and that was the beginning I suppose of my performing years.'

When Laurie Holloway lived in Trafalgar Street, he started to play the piano at the age of four years old. When he was seven, he started having lessons at 2/6 hour (13p) and by the time he was 13 had become the organist and choirmaster of his local Church. At 16 years old, he was offered a full time job in a dance band and began his successful and happy musical career. He has played and written for Cleo Laine and Judy Garland, among others and writes music for many T.V. shows, including Blind Date and Beadles About.'

Laurie Holloway and Marian Montgomery, married in Georgia, U.S.A., 1964.

'When I was chosen by the mill in 1932 to represent them in the Cotton Queen of Great Britain contest, all the neighbours were very excited. I worked at the Oldham Ring Doubling Company on Huxley Street and all the workers voted. Mrs Lord on Smyrna Street, made my dress. We lived on Roundthorn Road, and in those days your life belonged to everyone and when this posh Bentley came to pick me up and take me to Belle Vue, everybody was out of their houses watching, waving and cheering. I felt like the Queen and I suppose I was – that day – Queen of Glodwick that is! I suppose for an ordinary family like ours, it was special. There were six children in our house and it was only four roomed. Six of us kids slept in one room, Irene and me in a 3/4 bed, my brothers slept together – how they got three beds in that room beats me. Everyone was healthy, we never ailed anything – no central heating, when it was cold you just cuddled up'

'When Edna came home that day all the neighbours were excited for us – we lived on Hollins Road at the time – course at that time, we didn't know that she would become the 'Cotton Queen of Great Britain' at eighteen. We went to London and I'll always remember we had tea with the Lord Mayor – he said how proud he was to meet an Ambassador – our Edna, he meant, can you believe it!

She was a lovely girl and so clever, I don't know why she ever went in the mill. Her eyes were like stars – they sparkled!

Tom was an Australian who came over here during the war and although there were so many men after Edna, she finally married him, and went back to Australia. My mother said, "I feel I've lost her now".'

Above right: Edna Taylor, Cotton Queen of Great Britain marrying Thomas Hyde in Oldham during the war.
Left (inset): Edna Taylor, 1926.
Top left: The Crowning Cermony
Left: Cotton Queen Pageant, 1932

'We had all worked from being youngsters, we were still only in our early teens. Somebody must have said "come outside, I'll take your photo". We look quite happy I expect we were, we didn't know any different, we all look clean with shiny hair, must have been quite early morning, we had a lot of fettlin' in front of us.'
Right: Six 'little tenters' from the Roy Mill, Royton 1925. Ann Coleman, Olive Jones, Nellie Bodell, Edith Briggs, E. Stainthorpe and Lily Coleman.

Above Left:
Sir Cecil Wakeley, past
president of the Royal
College of Surgeons, with
Norman Stoller inspecting
one of the knitting
machines in 1962.

Above Right: Oldham
Central Library, before
open access.

The challenges that Setons faced in the beginning were tremendous. To educate people into a different way of thinking was an innovation in itself. For many years, there had only been one way of bandaging which could be traced back to Egyptian mummies – now here was someone coming along, who was going to alter all that!

'I suppose the first breakthrough came because of boredom whilst I was in Copenhagen in 1953/54. Because I was the world's expert (there was only one!) on tubular bandages, I decided to visit the largest hospital in Copenhagen and being ignorant of the system, asked to see the head of the hospital. Because the Danes at that time were very aware of the fact that British Forces had repatriated Denmark from German occupation, they had a great feeling of warmth and friendship towards them, and this was the real reason I was seen by the head of the hospital. This was the real

beginning of our export trade and developed a cash flow which allowed us to expand, and gain business and respect worldwide.'

'When we went to the library we had to stand in front of the counter and tell the librarian what we wanted and we had to point to a book in the glass enclosed shelves. I hated not choosing the right one, because you couldn't change your book the same day as you took it out. I thought it was absolute heaven to be able to wander round looking at any book that took my fancy. During the depression a lot of unemployed men frequented the reading room, partly because it was somewhere warm to be, I thought it was terrible, because the authorities – or whoever made the decisions– removed the racing news and sometimes it was even blacked out in the newspapers, and someone, an attendant I think, used to go round waking up anyone who had gone to sleep.'

Central Library, Oldham,
introducing open access.

FOR OF SUCH IS THE KINGDOM OF HEAVEN

Consider the lilies of the field, how they grow; they toil not, neither do they spin:
Even Solomon in all his glory was not arrayed like one of these　　　St. Matthew

Whit-Walks

The Whit-walks used to be seen as an event of great importance and significance. The local churches took this opportunity to exercise their self-respect – they were making a statement. With the bellied-out banners there was a firmness and a resolve, a renewed promise of faith for at least another year. The weather was of tremendous importance, all the saving up through the year and knowing that a good day would bring out the watching crowds, meant to some walkers that God was on their side.

'What used to make my Aunty mad was, we would meet at 10.15am and there would hardly be anyone watching. Also the buses were running – the traffic wasn't stopped. At approximately 11 am the traffic stopped and the Catholics walked – we loved it and wouldn't have missed it for anything the

bands with their rousing "Faith of our Fathers" and "The Wearing of the Green", bringing out the goose pimples. My Aunty would say the same every year "Who are all these people watching? Why didn't they turn out for their own?" I used to wonder about that – what was really meant by "their own" and you would see the young men walking and think, "I've been home with him, I didn't know he was a Catholic", as if it made him different in some way and when he glimpsed you, he would sort of look a bit shifty, because at that precise moment he knew you *weren't* a Catholic or you would be walking – so at that time, in the fifties it must have mattered.'

Above: Whit-Friday St. Mary's RC Church, coming up Yorkshire Street c1961.

Above Top: Whit-Friday c1952. Oldham Parish Church.

Whit-Friday 1947.

Oldham Citadel Band, 1938.

Below: Walking with the Wesleyan Chapel, in Derker in the 1930s.

Going past the Star Inn 1947.

Below: Westwood Moravians, 1954.

Below: Rhodes Bank, 1950s.

Below: Rose Queen retinue, Garden Suburbs, 1930.

Above top: Ward Street, Sunday School 1930s.
Above: Northmoor Methodist c1956 on Trafalgar Street.
Dunbar Street Catholic School is in the background.

'We had a cadet band and they used to drum and bugle to take a little mission round the streets on Whit Friday. It was George Johnson's Mission, up steps on the right hand side of George Street, and it rained one Whit Friday. It was an awful day, but they still turned out with their Queen and their little modest procession and after a service in Union Street Methodist to escape from the rain – at 10 minutes to eleven someone announced it was fine and they all came outside and the streets were lined with people waiting to watch the Catholics. An Oldham policeman ordered them to turn down Brunswick Street – he wanted them off Union Street, before St. Patricks came on it. I intervened and told them to carry on over Union Street. He threatened to book me – that little mission had only a few yards to go back to their Church – there was a lot of prejudice even from the police then.'

'I remember Whit-Walks – St. Mary's Roman Catholic School was on Cardinal St., and we used to come down from St. Stephens, they would bring their banner out across Horsedge Street to stop us getting down – course we had to stop . . . and the Vicar for St. Stephens – I mean this is going back 50 odd years – was up to fighting – with the Priest – it was daft – but that's how it was then.'

'Soon the streets were awash with the agitation of . . . restless youth and colour, the wind taking the banners and filling them out like sails, and making the veils to stream and the slender shepherd's crooks, tufted with posies, to sway like beds of blown flowers . . All round that animated picture the black facades of the town raised their monstrous unscalable walls, so that it seemed as though the exercise yard of a prison had for once been taken over for a riot of joy.'

from SHABBY TIGER
by Howard Spring

St. Annes School

*School days fly past all too
soon and we scatter
Knowing not whither life's
journey may end;
But of this we are certain
and naught else can matter;
'Oldham' – anywhere,
always means friend*

*There are golden days we
shall never forget,
And things to recall with
a pang of regret,
The lessons we've mastered
the matches we've won,
The work we've completed
or only begun*

School

'I suppose my lasting impression is one of total girlishness, wrestling with conscience. Although we had a mental toughness, we were very naive in terms of worldly wisdom. We were very trusting and there was an obsession with modesty and cleanliness. I know for a fact that my sister – and this would be in the 30s, when she was about eight years old – at the convent she went to they were bathed by a young nun, in turns, but they had to wear a swim-suit!'

'If you were off school poorly, you had to stay in – you weren't even allowed to stand at the door. On the last day, before going back to school, you were allowed to walk around the block or perhaps accompany someone to the store, but never any outings, the same later when you were working "If you are well enough to show your face, you're well enough to work!" Looking back, it seems that even minor and common illnesses like measles and mumps involved a more complicated ritual than is usual today.'

Greatness is not always largeness
Help the child to understand
Strength and skill are happy partners
It's the mind that guides the hand.

*Far Left: Northmoor
Council School 1928. Irene
Brooks – second from right
– on second row.*

*Left: Richmond Street
Infants 1930s.*

*Below: Oldham Parish
Church c1931.*

The New School Knicker

Lastex Yarn in waist and legs

THE enormous demand we have received for this new knicker (F.144) is indicative of its success and popularity among schools. It has several special features which appeal strongly to all who regard health with the importance it deserves. Instead of the usual elastic which frequently nips and interferes with healthy circulation, we have had a wide band of Lastex yarn knitted in the waist and legs. This clings in a most determined fashion, but without the slightest constriction or pressure. In between the legs, where so much of the wear comes, there is an extra large double gusset. Woven from a two-fold Botany yarn in navy, cream, brown, fawn and green.

Sizes			2	3-4	5-6	7-8
Ages			4-5	6-9	10-13	14-17
Wholesale prices			4 -	4 9	5 6	6 3
Retail prices			4 9	5 6	6 3	7 -

NOTE.—Wholesale prices are quoted for a minimum quantity of 48 garments delivered direct to the School.

Below Left: 'Rule Brittania', local school c. 1930s.

Below Right: Oldham High School Hockey team 1936-37.

In 1951, 'Janet and John' took over from 'Dick and Dora'. The activities in Janet and John books resembled everyday happenings, but the way learning differed most from today was the awareness of and preparation for the 'eleven-plus', when greater emphasis than ever before was placed on this be-all and end-all examination.

The General Certificate of Education (G.C.E.) was launched in 1951 to replace the old school certificate which had only been awarded if the candidate passed in at least five subjects.

'Someone from the Chron. came to take a picture of us in the school yard with our hoola-hoops. We all had one, it was a craze that seemed to last a long time. I think somebody said it was bad for your spine or something like that, but like all the crazes, it lasted until we got fed up with it. My hoop came from the Market Hall, they were all bright colours – everyone counted the number of rotations.'

Below: Pat Bradley on left, Sheila Greenhalgh next to her and Linda Hancock to the left of Sheila.

BELONGING

I promise on my honour . . . to do my best:
To do my duty to God, To serve the Queen,
To help other people at all times, and to obey the Guide Law.

When I was a very young Guide, I found one of the laws very hard to keep, it was: "A Guide smiles and sings under all difficulties". I used to think it expected a lot, and I didn't always feel like singing – or smiling when things went wrong as they occasionally do. Even so, I thought Guiding was wonderful and a tremendous character builder, definitely makes you learn to consider others.'

'I always knew that it was a big thing to belong to – when I was a Guide in the 60's there was about 6 million members all over the world. It was a way of life to follow through peace and war, prison camps, concentration camps, up mountains, across oceans, in skyscrapers, jungle huts and royal palaces. Even now I am older I am aware that the saying is very true "Once a Guide, always a Guide".'

'Some of the things a Guide had to be prepared for, now seem so ridiculous but a list from the Guide Handbook of 1970 which cost 7/6 (37^1/$_2$p) gives some of the duties expected.

- **Amuse a baby**
- **Carry six eggs**
- **Draw a sketch map**
- **Tie on a loose exhaust pipe**
- **Mop up a tearful child**
- **Cope with snapped knicker elastic**
- **Make a call from a phone box**
- **Keep a shoe on when the buckle has come off**
- **While away a long boring wait**
- **Temporarily fix badly torn trousers**
- **Chop kindling wood without chopping yourself**
- **Light your fire or boiler**
- **Unstop a sink**
- **Clean out a drain**
- **Throw a rope up to a high window**
- **Row a boat**
- **Pluck a chicken**
- **Put on a car handbrake**
- **Catch a fish**
- **Beat out a grass fire**
- **Replace a bicycle chain**
- **Catch a pony**
- **Identify mushrooms**
- **Bake bread**
- **Milk a cow**
- **Put a clean nappy on a baby**
- **Mend a puncture**
- **Clean a fish**
- **Sharpen a knife**
- **Dress in the dark**

Below: 1949 Guide camp

There must have been people who have been presented with their Duke of Edinburgh award and even people with the O.B.E. who haven't tackled half of those things. A lot was expected of Guides then, they were taught to be totally reliable and as self sufficient as was possible.

'There was an exhibition camp at Heathbank on Windsor Rd, which became the Spastics Centre. The exhibition ran for four days and was to commemorate Jubilee Year. It was open to the public and the standard was really high, only Guides who had already

'Mighty summits stretch
before me
Dwarfing every human thing,
Nature's glory, round me,
o'er me
Do you wonder that I sing?'
    – Girl Guide Song

*Below:Brenda Mutch at
District camp at
Greenfield. 'It has been
said that if you can camp
at Greenfield, which is on
a hill and couldn't be
wilder, you can camp
anywhere. One of the
wonderful things is, it is so
near Dick Clough, which
is the only place in
Oldham where you can
always hear the cuckoo.'*

camped were allowed to go. Every morning
the Guides would jog the length of Windsor
Rd. which was one mile. We had the most
super camp-fires when everybody joined in.
I'm sure many young women today will
remember it.'

'I think I was a terrible Guide. I never had
the proverbial piece of string in my pocket or
the paper and pencil. Instead I had a
lipstick, comb and mirror, I was never
prepared. I didn't like it raining on parade
and splashing my socks in the puddles or
getting my hair wet and generally looking a
drag – but I wouldn't have missed guide
night – not on your life. Scouts met on the
same night – perhaps that was a pull, but
not everything, I really loved Guides.'

'I eventually became a leader and we used to
have lots of fun on Guide night, I never knew
whether I did it the correct way. I took them
camping, before I got my licence – up at
Greenfield. I called a meeting of parents and
got them to make a list of the things the
children would need. Looking back now, those
Mums and Dads must have been a bit worried,
because I was so fancy and must have
appeared such a scatterbrain but they let them
come and we had an amazing time.

It was such a relief to get the tents up and
the orderly tent for the food. I must have been
ambitious because I made huge meat
puddings, like flock beds, in dixies and jam
sponge to follow. The custard at camp was
always scorched slightly, but everyone was so
hungry it was like nectar.'

'When the last torch glimmer has gone out
and you are up on a hillside, it is blacker
than anything you can imagine and one or
two younger guides would always creep into
your sleeping bag, they were so scared. It
was probably their first camp. I have had as
many as three little ones fast asleep and me
squashed hot and sweaty in the middle. I
think now – how times have changed and
through misguided information or whatever,
comforting situations like that would be
misinterpreted and it fills me with sadness.
My sleeping bag was a large old eiderdown,
stitched up on one side or I couldn't have
accommodated them all.

What, I thought, am I doing taking 16 little
guides camping? My pioneer spirit is
noticeably lacking. Putting tents up in
daunting rain, the wind lashing at bare legs,
I was aware of being too close to earth and
sky.'

*Oldham Sea Cadets at Holyhead in June,
during the Investiture of Prince Charles as
Prince of Wales. Royal Yacht in background*

The starting up of a Sea Cadet Unit in
Oldham came about initially because
England was at war. In 1942, the Chronicle
advertised a meeting to be held at Oldham
High School on Greengate Street. The war
was in its third year and England was
suffering rather heavy losses at sea. It was
probably thought that with proper training,
recruitment into the Royal Navy and
Merchant Navy would be easier. The first
intake was seventy boys who began to meet
twice a week. Lack of equipment did
nothing to deter their enthusiasm – there
was a waiting list to join right up to the end
of the war.

*Left: 115th Oldham
Scouts, Northmoor.*

In 1926 two companies of the Boys Life Brigade amalgamated to form one large organisation under the title 'Boys Brigade'. The number of companies increased steadily over the years and peaked in the mid 50s and early 60s when another 34 companies enrolled. More than 80 churches in the Oldham area have had a Boys Brigade Company.

In 1965, the Girl's Life Brigade which was founded in England in 1902, combined with the Girl's Brigade of Ireland formed in Dublin in 1893 and the Girl's Guildry, founded in Scotland in 1900, and became The Girl's Brigade.

Its aim is to help girls achieve a sense of responsibility and to discover a true enrichment in life, while becoming a follower of the Christian faith.

Above left: Every year the Life Boys held an event called a 'Sportagama', which was held at King Street Stores.

Above right: 1948 Boys Brigade Camp.

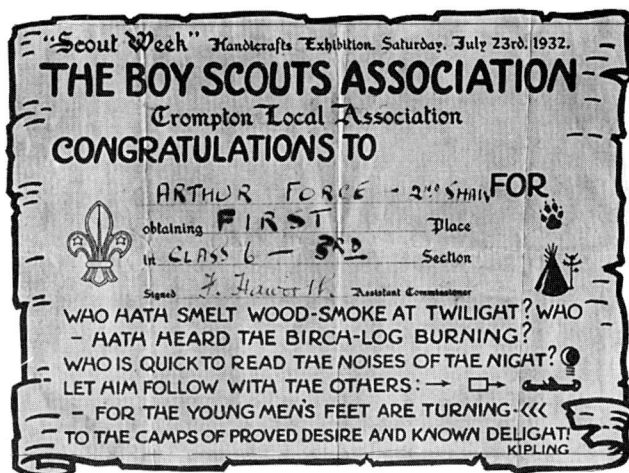

"Scout Week" Handicrafts Exhibition. Saturday. July 23rd. 1932.

THE BOY SCOUTS ASSOCIATION

Crompton Local Association

CONGRATULATIONS TO

ARTHUR FORCE - 2ND SHAW FOR

obtaining FIRST Place

in CLASS 6 - 3RD Section

Signed *J. Haworth* Assistant Commissioner

WHO HATH SMELT WOOD-SMOKE AT TWILIGHT? WHO HATH HEARD THE BIRCH-LOG BURNING? WHO IS QUICK TO READ THE NOISES OF THE NIGHT? LET HIM FOLLOW WITH THE OTHERS: FOR THE YOUNG MEN'S FEET ARE TURNING TO THE CAMPS OF PROVED DESIRE AND KNOWN DELIGHT!

KIPLING

Mount Pleasant Mission Girls Life Brigade on Union Street, 1941.

Left: on camping holiday c1940s
Below Left: Camping
Below: Cherry Clough
Below Right: Girl's Brigade, Bardsley Carnival 1961
Bottom: Cross country run, Shaw Cubs and Boys Brigade

Events, whether sad or happy, were never celebrated privately – they belonged to the whole immediate neighbourhood, and if help was necessary, as for instance at the birth of a baby or in some kind of misfortune, then the help was forthcoming. Families did not have much privacy but they didn't seem to want it.

Right: Wearing 'Sunday best' – the hats were inevitable c1929. The girls are Hilda and Marion Kidger, Clara Warwick, Lillian Roberts and Peggy Laister.

Below: Behind the scenes at St. Stephen's Church Bazaar which lasted for 3 days. Grandma Shaw in the centre used to cook and carve the turkey and Mrs. Hilton on the right was "boss of pots" in the 1930s.

'We all grumbled about going errands, we were too busy playing out but all children were sent on errands – the ploy of getting someone to go with you was always the same – you would share your rewards, could be an apple, a butty and sometimes only your friendship. I went often with a lad who had to make frequent visits to an official at the Town Hall to tell him that their tippler wasn't working; in due course a workman came to put it right. My impression is that they were very informal and more friendly than the bureaucrats of today'.

'No one in communities suffered illness or hardship without getting help from neighbours. It was one of the better known aspects of working-class life and was really authentic. Children also, had many others to answer to as well as their parents – they usually had a Grandma a few doors away, Aunties and Uncles in the next street and neighbours also were part of their extended family, so if they misbehaved, punishment and 'talkings to' came from every direction and seemed to keep them on the straight and narrow'.

Above top: A break from playing. Somewhere behind Middleton Road.

Right: Wakes Fair, Tommyfield 1938. Clogs were still in evidence.

Below: Cowboys and Indians in a backyard at Latimer Street.

Sybil Buckley on a lion in Alexandra Park.

*Osborne Street,
Coronation Party 1937.*

'Even though my father was a doctor, we didn't have a lot of money. It was expected that because of his position we would have a maid, but my mother did all her own washing and ironing. I remember, it was probably the end of the month, they would sit round the table and bills would be made out. It wasn't a wealthy practice – bills on average would be 6d a week – 1/– at the most and of course many people couldn't afford to pay and many of those doctor's bills were never paid. My mother used to help a lot.'

Below: 'We had about five nursemaids, they all came from Ireland and one by one they left, largely because they became pregnant. I mostly remember Delia, perhaps we gave her a hard time, but I recall once, I must have moved my leg when she was getting us ready and my shoe came off – she told me to put my finger in the electric socket and I got a shock. I remember being very frightened and aiming not to cross her after that.'

'In 1937 when we got a house to rent, my husband had a job but his wage was about £3 a week and what with bus fares etc., we had no money and yet my husband was lucky, because at least he was in work. The insurance companies at the time didn't employ married women so I had no job. I had to go before a tribunal before I could draw unemployment benefit – I lost my case, as did many other unemployed married women during that period'.

*Billiard Hall, Union St.
(Now Bingo Hall).*

Below: 'A vegetarian's nightmare' Winners of window dressing competition, 1930's

New Radcliffe Street. Children's Jubilee Tea Party

Townfield Coronation Tea Party

Above: Coronation party – Police Station 1937.
Right: Coronation Celebrations. Beever Street
School 1937.

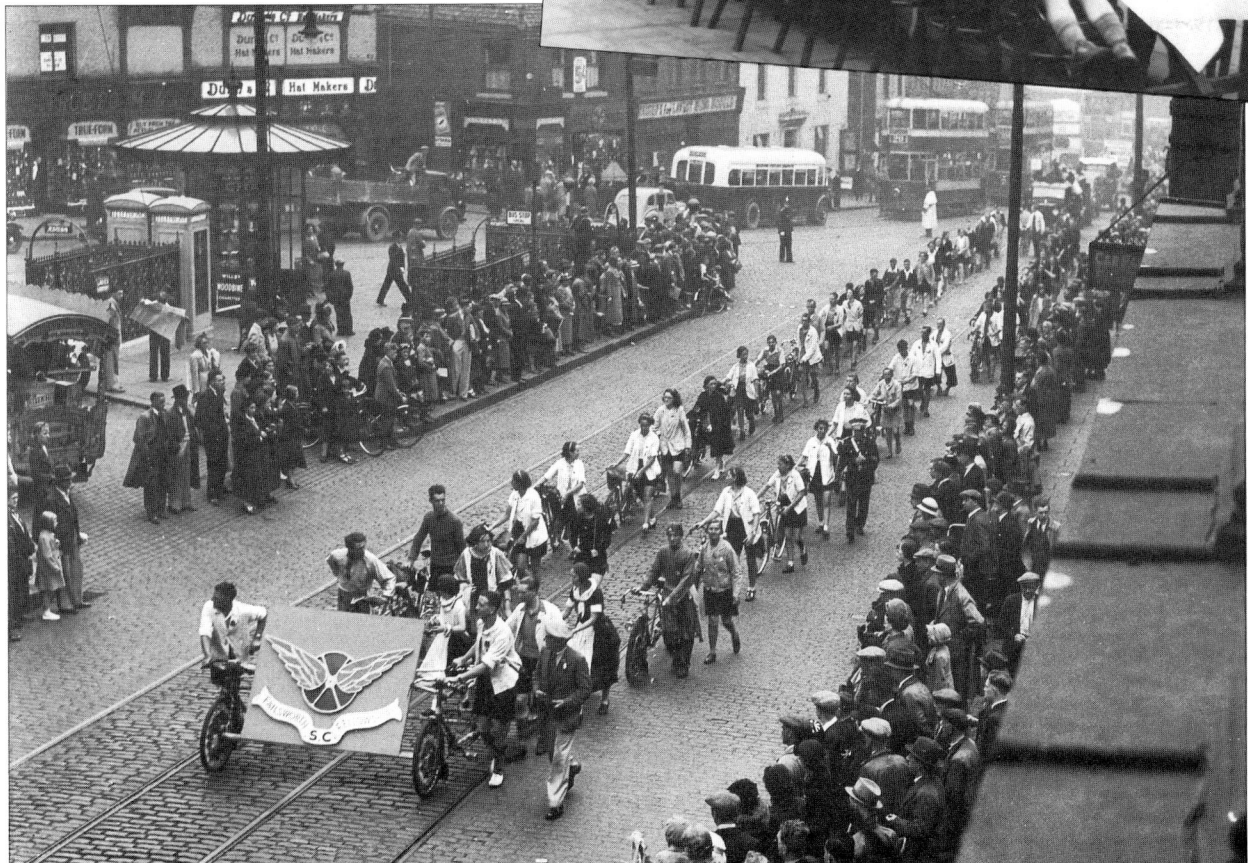

Horse and Cycle parade coming through Mumps 1938.

Left: Keith Andrew and his mother Gladys Andrew, Oldham 1940s. Keith, an Oldham boy who played cricket at Werneth, played for Lancashire, Northants and England before finally becoming Chief Executive at Lords.

'I used to practice catching by throwing a tennis ball at the rough brick walls of the gardens on Queen's Road and catching the rebound. This would happen all the way up to my grandmother's in Glodwick. I suppose I never realised at the time, how important this impromptu practise would prove to be.'

'The only wicket keeper that stood up to quick bowling apart from Godfrey Evans was Keith Andrew. I remember being in to bat and feeling threatened when it was Keith.'

Left: Darrell Shaw, playing table tennis at the Y.M.C.A. Darrell was County Lawn Tennis Champion – appeared several times at Wimbledon. Was Director of Shiloh Spinners.

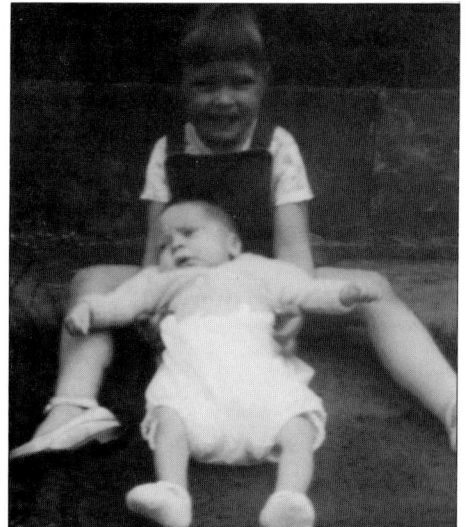

Anne and John Kirkbride at 134 Littlemoor Lane c1958

'When I came out of the Army, I kept looking for houses, to rent or buy, but so many people were house-hunting then. I went to put my name down at the Council – it was Mr. Pickering and I told him I had seen some new ones being built on Stoneleigh and I wanted one of those. I realise now he must have thought I was mad because he said. "Do you know they are queueing from here to Rhodes Bank for them?".

In 1958 it started, the people on Littlemoor Lane got notice that the whole area was going to be re-developed and the whole row of houses were going to be knocked down. It was our first home and we hated the thought. Eventually by 1959, we were the only family left, we still refused to move. We kept receiving bunches of keys and instructions to go and look at other properties which we didn't like half as much as ours, besides, we were surrounded with fields. What did it . . .a house became available on Oban Ave – it was handy for the kids as they both went to Derker School. It had an outside wash house and two toilets, one up and one down. We moved on New Years Day 1960 and eventually Anne went to Counthill and John to Hulme.

A few weeks after we had moved I went on a sentimental journey to look at the place we had left. There was just a pile of rubble and standing in the middle was our large cast-iron bath. It stood there for weeks like some great monument and I felt rather sad, it was the end of an era for our family. We had rented the house at first and then bought it as sitting tenants for £350 and we had put so much love in it.'

Queen Elizabeth (now The Queen Mother) visiting Oldham, meeting Joe Carr – the oldest operative at Stotts. Proctor Stott on her left, the Mayor on her right. Detective behind. c1950.

*Left: Punch and Judy,
Alexandra Park c 1950s.*

*Below left: 1953
Coronation Celebrations,
Atherton Street.*

*Below right: Young people
from Zion Methodist setting
off on an Easter hike early
1950s.*

*Left: Feeding the ducks,
Alexandra Park c 1955.*

*Below: Large crowd to
watch Wigan play Oldham
at Watersheddings c1950*

*Queueing for coke
February 1951.*

*Coal picking at
Bellfields, Hathershaw
in January 1951.*

*The summer of 1953. Children playing in Jabez Bath,
Greenfield. This is now covered by Dovestone Reservoir.*

'We were forever climbing and jumping from the top of the outside toilets onto the wall from house to house, people used to knock on the windows, and say the bobby would get us, but we had no fields or meadows to play in.'

MAKING A LIFE

'We walked a lot when we were courting, it was the cheapest form of courtship. We saved up for a year for the ring. I remember one night we were almost too stiff and cold to move, we had been sat down on a form in the park for so long.'

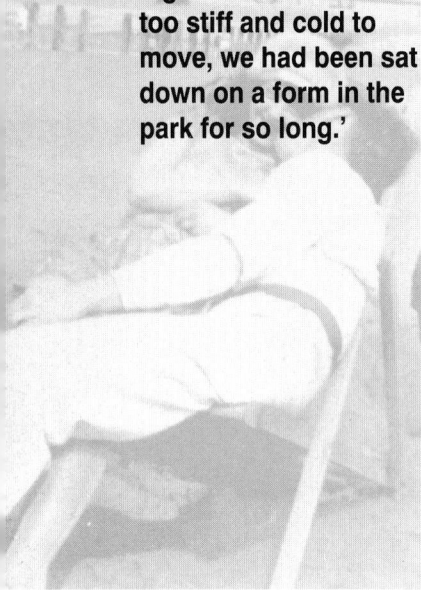

Above: Courting, Blackpool

Below left:Marian Bell and Charlie Jones, courting, just before the 2nd World War.

Courting

'She fell for my "civi" suit. It was a new one – a demob. suit. I fell for her blue-black hair. It was really nice. Whenever I see long hair, I always have to stop and admire it, I've always said "a woman's hair is her crowning glory".'

"Time he were going – he's been here long enough." They insisted they see my boyfriend – they said " we must let him know what's what; we are having none of this hanky panky late at night." We were never allowed to go anywhere on our own – not even to the pictures. I had to be in for 10 pm, so it was impossible.'

'Her mother came. She said, "you'd better come over; she's poorly. She's having a nervous breakdown I think." I did go down. She was in bed – she was faking I think. They let me go in the bedroom to my surprise! Anyway, after that they let us go out more together – perhaps twice a week.'

42

'You always had a single room when you were courting and you went away together, and I remember once, I must have overslept one morning and my boy-friend came to see where I was. When I opened the door I said "I hope nobody has seen you come up here, (I was in the attic) don't put one foot in this room." I know it sounds ridiculous now, but I wonder if we were all frightened of having to get married.'

'When my mother had died my father was very strict – he wouldn't let me go anywhere, only to night school. By this time I had met Wilmer at Stotts and he used to bring me home, but I couldn't tell my father. Anyway he found out, because he would come and look for me and it was only 9.30 pm. Sometimes I would suggest to my friend that we went to Hill Stores or Froggatts – but I still had to be home for 9.30pm on a Saturday night. He went mad when he knew I was meeting a boy and he took me down one Sunday morning to see Wilmer's parents, he was so disgusted. It didn't make any difference, my father still wouldn't have him in the house – he said when I was eighteen I could bring him in – then I was only sixteen. I think if my mother had been alive things would have been different.'

'It was an understood thing that you behave yourselves. In fact the word sex was never mentioned. I think the only time we were tempted was when his mother and father were out on Sunday evenings – but we didn't do anything.'

Left: Aunty Beatrice and Uncle Jack Buckley courting on holiday c1938

Below: 'When we had this photograph taken at Rowlands on King Sreet, nobody knew we were courting. We just fancied having our photo taken together, but one day it was in the window and I had to go in the shop and ask them not to put it in the window – they probably thought it was very strange – but I was frightened of my father seeing it – or someone telling him.'

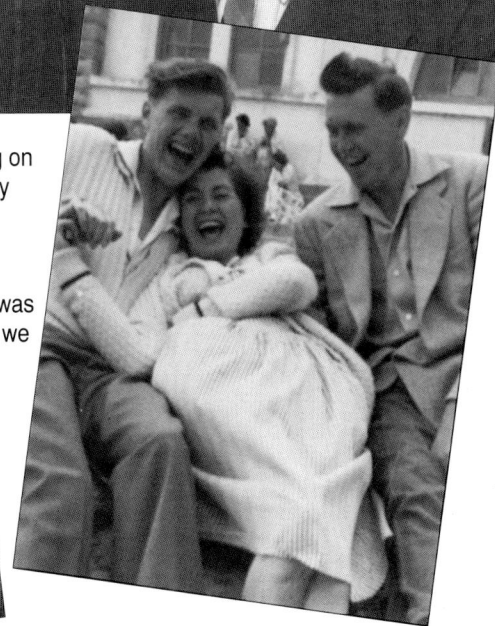

'When we were courting and were going on holiday, getting single rooms wasn't easy and one letter we got back offered one room with two beds and a curtain in between. We didn't take it, in fact we showed the letter all round the office. It was a real joke. It sounds strange today, but we weren't even tempted.'

Above Edith Standhaven and Fred Treadwell c1932.

Left 'Courting's a funny thing, if you went out with someone on a Friday, they said you were 'courting' – and if you took them home and they got their feet under the table – well that's it – you might as well call it a day. None of this, calling for you, going in for a coffee and all that like they do now. If they met the family it was serious.'

Something old,
Something new,
Something borrowed
and something blue

Harold Wilkinson and Emily
Kirkbride at Saint Mary's
Roman Catholic Church
October 1928.

Getting Married

Monday for wealth,
Tuesday for health,
Wednesday the best day
of all,
Thursday for losses,
Friday for crosses,
And Saturday, no luck
at all.

'It is evident that man, possessing reasoning faculties, muscular power and courage to employ it, is qualified for being a protector: the woman, being little capable of reasoning, feeble, timid, requires protection.
Under such circumstances, the man naturally governs; the woman as naturally obeys.'
'Infidelity and Divorce'
1840

The 1662 version of the marriage service uses the vow 'to love, cherish and obey'. After 1928, another version allowed 'obey' to be omitted.
'What matters it, O man that they
The marriage promise to obey
Should leave unspoken?
. . . A million women who have said
They would – soon after they were wed
Their vows have broken!'
Nowadays a wedding can take place anytime between 8am and 6pm – but before 1885, it was not possible to marry after midday. Soon after this, the government introduced an extension of three extra hours . . however, because of religious festivals in the Church i.e. Lent and between Rogation and Whit, at one period there was only 32 weeks out of the 52 in which people could marry in spiritual and mental ease and even then some thought was given to the day.

Jessie Taylor and Sydney Stott's wedding 1925. Married at Zion Chapel, Lees – the day that Woolworths opened.
Dress cost 30 shillings and the flowers were from Gartside's florists at Mumps.
Reception was held at Whitehead's cafe, Market Place.

Above: In the 1930s it was considered the height of fashion to either wear or carry a fur at a wedding, summer or winter.

Above: William Holland 'showing off' for his new wife on honeymoon at Blackpool 1929.

'I was 16 when I met Tom at Froggatts – he was on Embarkation leave. I went home with him and my mother had warned us that much about soldiers, but he was different. I went home with him about three times more before he went back to North Africa. He wrote to me and we got serious. He sent his sister the money to get me an engagement ring and those were very difficult to get at the time. Tom's sister and I queued about six hours for a ring – I didn't get one – the day after she queued on her own again and got me one.

It was another four years before I saw him again and he came home for 4 weeks leave. I felt nervous seeing him. My dad was just going to the pub and came running back. He said, "There's a fella coming up here, I think it's yon mon coming home". I didn't really know him you know; it was all done by letters. He wanted to get married and had to come and talk to my dad. I can see it now. The doorbell rang and I ran through to the kitchen – it was awful. My Dad stood with his back to the fireplace. "Well do you think you'll be able to keep her?" The wedding was arranged in 2 weeks, because he had to go back afterwards. The dress – everybody rallied round with the coupons. You couldn't be choosy; you had to get what you could. Everybody borrowed that dress – Annie Camps and a girl from Roundthorn Road, Eileen Douglas and Edith Lever and also Joan Boardman. It pulled on some, trailed on some but they were glad to have it, because it was every girl's dream to be married in white.'

'I had these stockings wrapped up in tissue, saving them for my wedding. I kept getting them out and having a peep. My father used to say 'Look well, if that's all you're going to

have to be married in! We had to buy a lot of second hand furniture. Mother gave us some sheets which we dyed rose pink for curtains. Everything was passed on from friends and neighbours, we had linoleum and rugs.'

'Everybody would say, "Where are you going for your 'first night?'". It was all that – it really was a first night for most of us. We were all afraid of having babies before we were married, and of course there was no pill. Strange as it may seem, in this pill-less generation, there was very little divorce.'

Below left: War time wedding – Joyce and Tom Plant.

Below: Joyce Kenworthy and Arthur Hibbert's wedding. 'In 1942, Arthur was going abroad and wanted us to get married, I bought a blue suit and a burgundy hat from Elizabeth Waltons at Mumps. We had Hibberts in Lees to cater for us at Springhead Conservative Club, but we had no money for a honeymoon. He came home just once on leave for a weekend and then I didn't see him for 3^1/$_2$ years.'

'We had this house on Shaw Road in Royton and it belonged to my boyfriend's parents, who had a shop on Middleton Road. We got married before he went in the forces because the war was on. I got the material for my dress from Affleck and Brown's in Manchester and a lady on Shepherd Street made it. Everything then – you had to have coupons for – but if you were getting married, people would give you a few coupons to help. For weeks and weeks before, we asked everybody – if they had any food coupons to spare would they let us have them to give to the people who were doing the reception.'

In 1938 there were 409,000 marriages in the U.K. . . . but numbers escalated. By 1939 the number was 495,000 and 534,000 by 1940. It didn't rise again until the war ended in 1945.

Florence Brazel and Thomas Dunkerley.
'The bride wore pale pink slipper satin with matching shoes and the bridesmaids had pale blue. Thomas, however, wasn't allowed to enter the Church by the front door because he wasn't a Catholic. The wedding was on Primrose Day which commemorates the death of Disraeli.'

'I got married in 1940, I went to the 'Guinea' shop in Manchester for my dress and I was six coupons short, so the lady said she would save it for me, until I could cadge some coupons off anyone and eventually I went and collected it. We didn't have any photographs taken, the main thing was, we had a house, it was lovely. I really loved that house on Wallace Street, I used to polish the windows so much that you couldn't see in – they shone and you could see your reflection. I think your first home is always a treasured memory. We had utility furniture, it was hard to polish – you know when the sirens went, I was more worried about my house than myself.'

'On the way to being married that morning the sirens went and we had to run in the shelter. After about half an hour when the all clear hadn't sounded we decided to go to church anyway, but the Minister wasn't there, and neither was anyone else. We got married 3 hours later, but it wasn't a bit as I imagined my wedding would be – the church windows were boarded up and we had no photographs.'

Evelyn and Harry Lees on honeymoon

'I was a virgin when I got married, I had said to Harry "I'm not having any messing about until God gives me permission in Church." All the films we had seen would end or fade with a kiss, we were brought up on romance and I don't think it did us any harm. In 'Gone with the Wind', Rhett Butler picked Scarlett O'Hara up and carried her up the stairs, but you didn't see anymore – it was left to your imagination.

The house, which was on Chadderton Rd., cost £375, Harry had been giving me a bit of money out of his wage every week and we saved up for the things we needed. The house had an old slopstone sink, an old sett boiler, a black iron fireplace, I suppose it was a mess really, but I was proud of that house, I loved it, it was our palace. I crocheted curtains out of Jimmy Stott's weft for the bedroom and the kitchen, and the boss caught me and made me undo one.

On our wedding night the lady next door was waiting for us and I invited her in (she probably wanted to have a nosey anyway) we sat talking for ages, because I was scared to death of going to bed with Harry. The stairs came into the kitchen and he went up and I sat on the third stair for a long time. We had no inside toilet, so I put the chamber pot in the back bedroom and I was trying to wee without him hearing me and I put the light out before I got undressed.'

Above left top: Reuben Godfrey and Jane Brierley (sitting) 1928.

Above left: Bertha Curley and Harold Brooks, 1930s.

Above right: John and Elsie Hirst, 1930.

Left: Josie Bottoms and Harry Bottomley, Queen Street, 1928.

Below left: Beatrice Iles, 1930s. She had a gown shop on Yorkshire Street.

Below right: Dorothy Broadbent and Chadwick Middleton at Bourne Street Methodist, 1937.

Marjorie Williams and Alan Wolstencroft at St. Thomas's, Coppice

Olga Cunliffe and Peter Bradbury Christ Church Glodwick – 1950s.

Marcus Holloway and Alice Davenport's wedding, June 9th 1945 at the Wesley Chapel, Greenacres Road.

Above: Jimmy and Joyce Bennett's wedding 1947. Oldham Parish Church.

Above: Gladys Finney arriving at Northmoor Methodist for her wedding to Bill Farrow.

Left: Dora Bryan and Bill Lawton's wedding at St. Thomas's, Coppice. 1953. The bride wore dusky pink.

Harry Hirst and Joan Valentine, married in Colwyn Bay at Joan's local church in the 1940s.

Below: Vera Kelsall and Robert Hyatt at St. Thomas's, Coppice, 1953.

Above: Jessie, Irene Whatmough and Alice Broadbent at Hilda Whatmough's wedding in 1935.

Above: Sybil Buckley and Kenneth Curley, 1948.
'My suit was made by Beatrice Iles. Hat 4gns from Flacks, but they wouldn't let me bring it home – I put a deposit on it, it was pale blue feathers. I had tan leather shoes and suede gloves. My flowers were white lilac and pink roses from Cloughs on the Hill and a friend of ours, brought some nylons from Germany.'

Above: Geoffrey Heathcote and Jean Landregan, Northmoor Methodist, 1956.

John & May

Above: Courting. On holiday with relatives.

Above top: May and John with nephew Roy.

'I saved up, it was very hard, but I got enough together to buy a motor bike, and I used to play cricket on Bellfields. I got talking to May's brother Jack, who also had a bike and that's how I first met May – she was only 14 – and we started going out, with a few at first and then on our own.'

'I had to be in at 10pm every night and we were engaged then. If I was late I was banned from going out the rest of the week. Although I was engaged I only got 1d in the 1/– pocket money.

I got my dress from London fashions on Oldham Street, Manchester. My sister borrowed the veil for me from somebody at work. My cousin made the bridesmaids dresses.

We had the reception at the Lark on Hollins Road. We cadged meat coupons from our relations and the local butcher saved us an ox-tongue.

We went to Paignton for our honeymoon, which was a bit ambitious in war time. When we were walking to Hollinwood with our suitcases, a man stopped us and gave us a lift – he must have seen John in uniform. He took us all the way to Manchester. People were like that during the war, they all helped each other.

Many soldiers had no home to come back to after the war and we were no different. We lived with my parents for a while, but we had our name down on the housing list. We eventually got a pre-fab for 12/6 a week, No. 5 Tweed Close and we were thrilled to bits.'

Left: Tweed Close off Chamber Road.

Right: May and Stephen

Having Babies

'Until I had children, I had a deep political awareness. When troubles arose on ideological grounds in other parts of the world, I was able to give real objective thought to it; what threats it carried for mankind as a whole, I could think logically, but when you bear children you become afraid *for them.* I remember when my second baby was born, my first thought, all mixed up with the undoubtable pleasure of having another baby was "Oh no! I've done it again." There he lay, another small individual who I was – from now on, responsible for, it is emotional bondage, that's what it is.'

'When I started to show I used to keep looking at my reflection in shop windows, I was so thrilled and excited about having a baby and by that time I had stopped being sick. Towards the end I was enormous and the clinic at Boundary were always shoving me on the scales to see if I was putting too much weight on. I wasn't unduly bothered, I suppose I thought if there isn't much room inside, it has to show outside and I only had 34" hips anyway. I was so enormous at the end (and twins had been ruled out with an X-ray) I had difficulty on a bus, because nobody could get past me in the aisle, but I felt wonderful and I had never looked better in my life.'

Give you greetings, o my children, you whose race has just begun,
You with eyes that shine like morning, you shall well and truly run,
You are mine to shape and fashion, you are mine to love and tend,
You are mine to give you courage
that you come to glorious end.

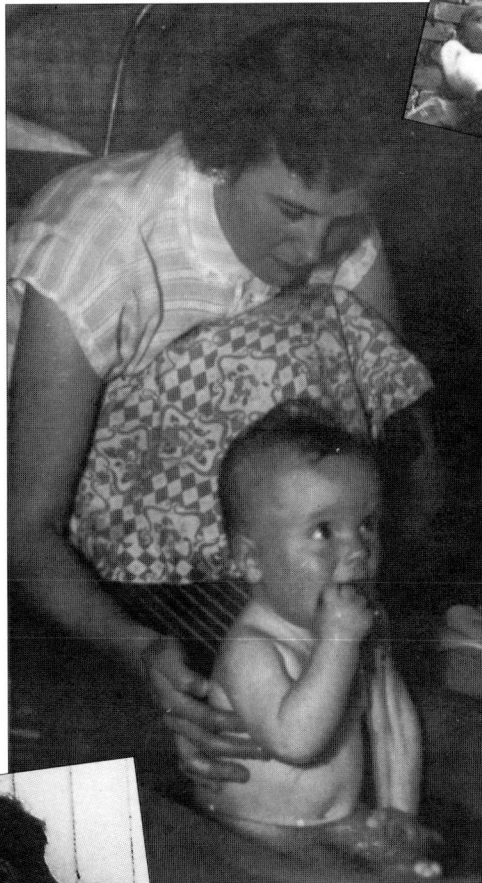

Above top: Sybil Curley with Martin.
Above: 'Bathnight on the rug' Betty Foden and John c1958.

'I went to have my first baby in Greenacres Lodge – you had to pay to go in there, it was a private nursing home – before Woodfield. When I started in labour I was terrified, I had absolutely no idea of what would happen. I hadn't read anything – there was very little information about having babies then – you only heard the old-wives tales and you were warned not to listen. I always remember, there was a girl across from me in Greenacres who wasn't married and she didn't want to keep her baby and after hours of labour I lost mine, I couldn't help but feel the injustice of it, I really wanted that baby.'

Above: Baby Show at Werneth Park c1932. Twins Beatrice & Edna, front row centre.

Below: Foxdenton Park 1962.

'There is such a lot of talk today about bonding. It was never mentioned in the 60s . . if it had been I would have been worried, wanting to be the perfect Mother and all that. I felt so ill after the caesarean and I remember them wheeling the baby in and handing her to my husband, who cried and said it was the most wonderful moment in his life. He said to me "Would you like to hold her?" and I said "No thank you" – how about that for bonding? I think love grows and with your baby, that love is so overwhelming.'

'I had read about natural child-birth and how easy it was if you got the breathing right, so I went to relaxation classes, never missed one, even in a blizzard, I was the only one there because I walked. What a shock it was and a disappointment when after being hours in labour I had to have an emergency caesarean section. I didn't realise the significance of the doctor's questions when he picked one of my slippers up and asked me the size of my feet, which were $2\frac{1}{2}$ – I thought he was just being friendly . . I was so confident. Labour was a shock, I admit, I remember thinking that it was the best kept secret in the world!.'

'If you were sure the birth was going to be uncomplicated, it was more fashionable to go into Woodfield Maternity Home on Manchester Road. To go into Woodfield you actually went for an interview, after you had first been to your G.P. You had to stay in 10 days – you provided everything for yourself and your baby, except the nappies. The best thing about Woodfield was *afterwards* – you had afternoon tea on a tray and everything was nicely presented. Two years later when I had my second baby, I didn't need to take anything in, everything was provided, and that time I only stayed in 7 days, but it was a wonderful rest after you have had a baby to be pampered a bit.'

In the early twenties, Marie Stopes, a British doctor and the wife of A.V. Roe, the aeroplane designer, publicly advocated birth control. She met with strong opposition, and although her arguments were sound, pointing out the advantages of fewer children, it wasn't until the end of the decade that methods of contraception were recommended by doctors and contraceptives appeared, albeit discreetly, in chemist's shops.

'We didn't say anything for a bit when I found I was pregnant, because we hadn't been married long – then we told my mother-in-law, who wasn't pleased at all – so that spoiled it a bit. When I was 32 weeks, the doctor sent me for an x-ray – they had no scans then, and it appeared there was something wrong and I had to go in. Mr. Steptoe showed Brian the X-rays and I had to go into labour knowing that my baby was going to be still born, I was in floods of tears. I never saw the baby, they didn't ask me if I wanted to and I was shuffled from ward to ward, once over I was even on the corridor – it was never talked about, I suppose they

thought it might upset the other mothers, but it was a very lonely experience.'

'When you lose a baby, there is grief and instead of getting congratulation cards, the people at work sent me 'get well' cards – rather than ignore it completely and of course – just to let me know they were thinking of me. The cards were all on the window-ledge and the midwife came in one day and she knocked them all down and she said "You are not *ill,* you've had a baby!" Of course when she went out I started to cry. Attitudes have changed since then thank God – the midwife could not understand what I was crying for.'

'We went on a course for engaged couples organised by the Catholic Church – they talked about things like the 'safe period". By the time I had my second baby who cried a lot I thought "Oh no!, I can't go through this again" and by that time the temperature method was introduced and we did go to the Catholic Marriage Guidance Council and we were told to take your temperature every morning and that would tell you if you were ovulating and give you a sign when to abstain. It wasn't very satisfactory so if it was the fertile time we used to use condoms, because whether you are a Catholic or not you have to think of your family and your health.'

'When I became pregnant again my second baby was $2^1/_2$, so I was delighted and then I lost the baby, I miscarried but I was more determined than ever to have another baby and I lost yet another. I gave the impression of being very brave, but I wasn't really, I screamed at the injustice. I had now lost 3 babies.'

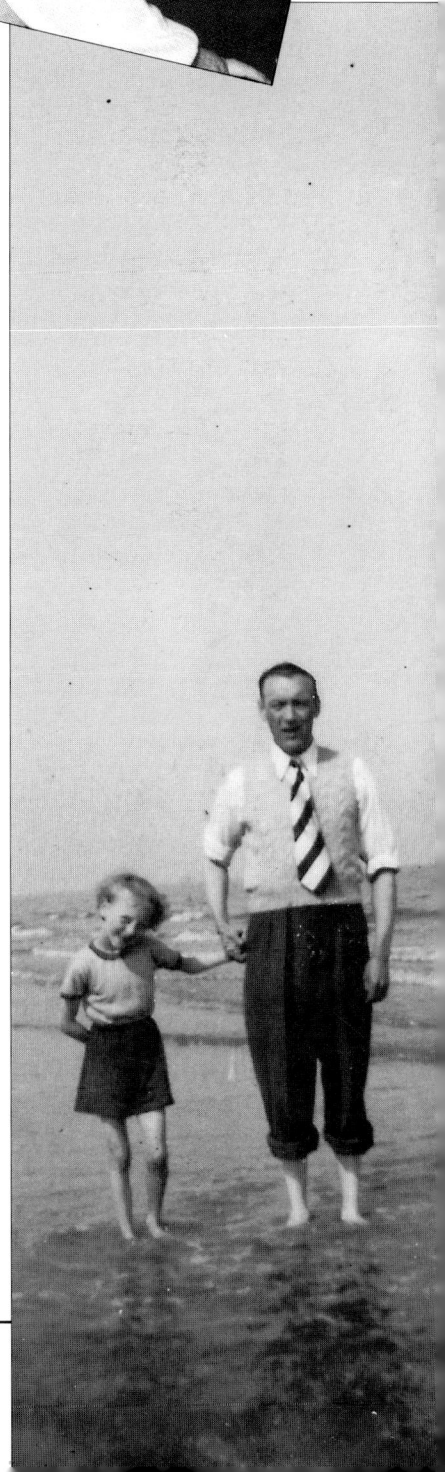

Having a paddle with Dad

TIMES OF WAR

The funeral of Germans due to be buried in Gibraltar. These men had been bombed by Spanish planes in the Spanish Civil War. Funeral by courtesy of the British.

'We crossed the Pyrenees in total darkness and when morning came you couldn't believe the drop – what a journey that was. We had been walking on the edge of a precipice, 300 ft deep. We were told to get in single file and put your arm on the person's shoulder in front of you and stay that way. In the daylight I could see why – we couldn't see the drop when it was pitch black.'

The Spanish Civil War

Although half of the world's press carried headlines to the effect that General Franco's forces had marched into Spain, the majority of the Oldham people knew very little about the implications of this move. To a cotton town like Oldham, Spain seemed a long way away in July of 1936. Besides there were a lot of happenings right on their own doorsteps.

The Grand Theatre had just been bought by Gaumont British and a new cinema – the Odeon was due to be opened in August by the Mayor. 4,000 people had watched cricket when Royton played Rochdale. Plans for a new maternity block at Boundary Park Hospital and a new fire station had been approved. Soon it would be Oldham Wakes and the exodus to the seaside would begin.

'There was a big discussion round the table, and heated arguments and my Grandpa's face was very red, so much so that I thought it might burst any minute causing his eyes to fly everywhere and it was something to do with sanctions and the government's reluctance to use them against Italian aggression. I know that, while they were all arguing we had three lots of trifle and nobody noticed, oh yes, I think they must have been interested in politics to a certain degree.'

The local papers carried very little information about the happenings in Spain, but it was enough to fire the indignation of 10 young men from Oldham who decided to join the International Brigade. Although boredom and disillusionment caused by the depression was one reason, political idealism was also a spur.

The Spanish Civil War has been described by some as a dress rehearsal for the Second World War, but even though some sophisticated weapons were tried in battle for the first time, the volunteers had neither uniforms nor weapons and once they crossed the channel, the journey to Spain across the Pyrenees was long and arduous.

When the Oldham Chronicle stated in July 1936 'Abyssinia appeals for money, thousands of homeless and hungry – wounded and blinded by poisonous gas and incendiary bombs', people began to be concerned without losing their trust in the government.

Mr Baldwin, who was the Prime Minister at the time, was reticent about the Spanish situation, while Neville Chamberlain, the Chancellor of the Exchequer assured the British People that Germany and Italy didn't want war.

1939

In September 1939, the unthinkable became the inevitable and Europe was afire again a mere 21 years since the end of the war to end all wars.

Most people were away on holiday as the outbreak of war slowly approached. It was Oldham Wakes, which was then the last week in August and people in guest houses and hotels were each evening gathered round the wireless, hoping against hope that it was just a scare.

'There was a lady staying at Mrs Qualteroughs in Douglas, I.O.M. and she kept crying. I was too young to realise the consequences of the event of war happening, but I was told later that she was German and she must have been very worried about what would happen to her in that event.'

As eagerly as people had packed up for their holidays, they hurriedly packed up to return home. It was felt that they had to travel as soon as possible or they would be marooned.

'The boat back was crowded and where usually there is an obvious division between 1st class and Steerage nobody was bothering. Already the class barriers were down. There were hardly any lights on the boat and when we got into Fleetwood, none were visible from the shore, it was eerie and rather frightening. It wasn't quite dark, how it would have been in the pitch black I can't imagine. There were crowds of people at Central Station when we got off the train, many of them still praying that war wouldn't happen.'

'They were all at the kitchen window, my Gran, my aunties and the lady next door – it is a picture that I have never forgotten – all their faces framed somehow in that window, looking at us kids so sorrowfully, while we sat in the sunshine in the back garden dipping spanish in kali as the last minutes of peace ebbed away. I can't remember anything clearer than that about any other part of the war.'

Above: The last few days of peace. War would touch on the lives of many of these people. Wakes on the Tommyfield August 1939.
Left: Holidaying on the Norfolk Broads, Oldham Wakes 1939. 'War declared the morning after we came home.' Alice, Edgar, Molly, Dorothy and Chad.

Below: Probably one of the first queues of the war It was Monday, September 4th – the day after war was declared. They were queueing for blackout material at Pollards, on Union Street.

Above: Mill Street. Sandbagging the Police Station.
Left: Filling sandbags at Fleetwood in 1939.
Below inset: The recruiting office in 1939 for the
Royal Tank Corps. It was a temporary building and
the average number of recruits each day was about
twenty.
Below: Oldham people off on their last holiday in
peace-time, suitably clad in their best hats, coats
and trilbys and oblivious that on their return in one
weeks time, they would hear Chamberlain announce
"This country is at war with Germany".

Just before war was declared! Perhaps the man looking worried on centre of photograph has just heard the news and was wondering if the threat of war could be avoided. This was Oldham Wakes 1939 which was then the last week in August.

Oldham Wakes – Tommyfield 1939. The two boys in centre would eventually do their National Service.

'When war was declared, I was on holiday with my friend at Heysham Towers. We were told we had to go home as soon as possible – somehow, although we were having a good time, we wanted to go home. We must have been a bit nervous. We couldn't get straight to Oldham and had to go to Manchester, which was all in darkness. The buses had tiny blue lights and the police had tannoys, telling everyone where the nearest shelter was. Everyone thought we were going to be bombed immediately.'

'Never once did it occur to me that we might lose the war. I was ten years old and more happened to me in those six years than at any other time in my life. During that time I would grow up – go into long pants, play for Oldham school boys at football, start my first job, discover romance, lose my father and meet the girl I would eventually marry. Hiroshima brought it all to an end – but Hiroshima was a long way from Oldham on Saturday nights – the Savoy, and the Odeon on Sundays.'

Evacuees 1939.

Evacuees arriving.

Evacuees

Wars had always begun with partings and in September 1939 the Government made an announcement. It referred to the evacuation of school children. Heavy hearted mothers had only 24 hours to organise everything and take their precious cargo to an assembly point. Oldham families were not departers, they were only receivers and it became largely the responsibility of the W.V.S. to find homes for evacuees coming into Oldham from the cities. The problem of how well an evacuee would suit a particular home didn't arise.

The W.V.S. (Women's Voluntary Service) has its noble place in the annals of the civil defence in the second world war.

In London during the air-raids they were considered angels of mercy, but their missions were not confined to the cities. Much of their work was unspectacular, but vital to the war effort just the same. – like darning 38,000 pairs of socks weekly for the forces. They were responsible for the evacuation of 750,000 children, 542,000 mothers with babies, 12,000 expectant mothers and 77,000 others, including blind and invalid people, in just four days.

Herbert Morrison, who was the Home Secretary at the time, said about them: 'I would say that they consist of one million magnificent women who are simply applying the principles of good housekeeping to the job of helping to run their country in its hour of need. They are doing it under sometimes heartbreaking conditions – it is their distinctive and womanly contribution. It is something that no man could do, and something that the whole nation will not forget."

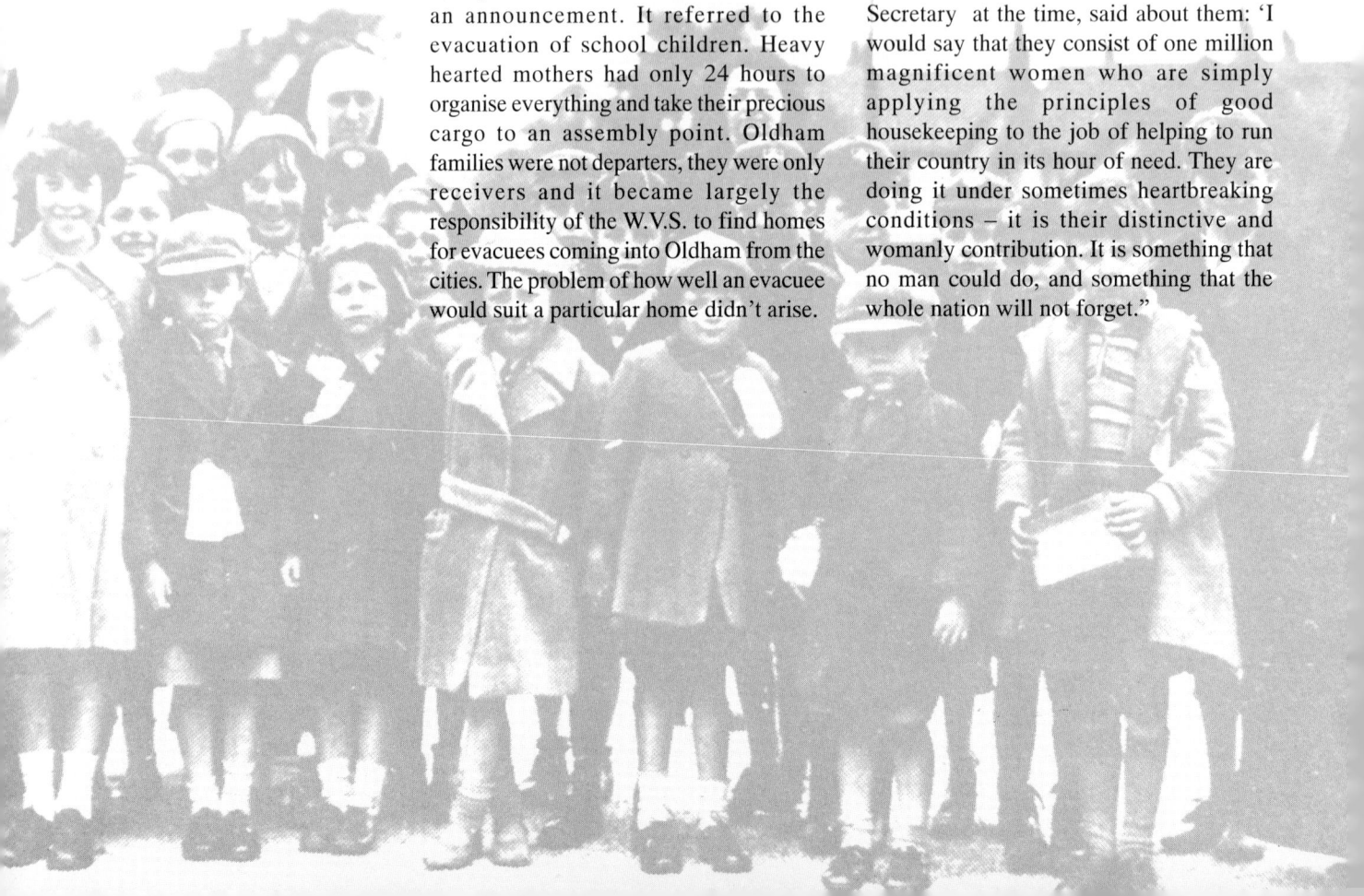

Whistling "We Don't Know Where We're Going Until We're There," nearly 800 evacuee children from the London area arrived in Oldham on Monday afternoon. They were met at Mumps Station by a civic party including the Mayor and Mayoress (Alderman and Mrs. Roberts), the Chief Constable (Mr. W.E. Schofield), Alderman Chamberlain, Councillor Graham, Mrs. MacInnes (W.V.S. organiser), Mrs. Clarke (Regional Organiser W.V.S.), Mr. H. Wrigley, (Billeting Officer), Mr. L. Fenton, representatives from the Health Office, and several others. The organisation was first-class and the children were quickly taken by special buses to Greenacres Co-operative Hall, King Street Co-operative Hall, and rest centres at Smith Street Methodist School, Derker Congregational, King Street Methodist and Union Street Methodist where a hot meal was served. Here, members of the W.V.S. the Civil Defence and other voluntary organisations helped to make the children comfortable.

An ambulance was outside the station in case of accident or illness, and one little boy was taken to hospital for observation. All the children were in high spirits and accompanied by teachers, were clutching their cases, parcels of clothing, dolls and toys as they moved to the waiting buses. After a meal and a rest at the centres they were medically examined before being placed in private billets.

The evacuees left St. Pancras at 9.30 in the morning and reached Oldham shortly before four o'clock. All were labelled. One small girl asked the Mayor, "What sort of place is this?" and was most interested to know there were picture halls and theatres, parks, etc., but was sorry there wasn't an open air swimming pool. A tiny six-years-old boy asked with a hopeful look in his eyes, "Are there any schools near here?" and seemed rather disappointed to learn that there were.

The ages of the children are from five to fourteen. Approximately one hundred of the evacuees were taken to billets on Monday night after they had been medically examined. Offers to billet the children are still coming in well but some more are still required.

The authorities are hoping to have fixed all these children up by tomorrow, but it is expected that more children will be sent to Oldham shortly. In other towns receiving evacuees, compulsion has not had to be resorted to and it is hoped that Oldham will respond equally well.

Local newspaper article.

They are now known as the *W.RoyalV.S.* – an honour bestowed on them because of their service to the Community.

It wasn't until June 1940 that Oldham was chosen as the haven for the boys from a school in Guernsey.

The complete collapse of the French Army on the 19th of June 1940, meant the Germans were advancing further and further west until they reached the French Atlantic coast. When the Nazis occupied Cherbourg it was generally felt that the Channel Islands would surely be invaded. After only 24 hours hundreds of children, many of them bewildered and afraid, were assembled at the harbour in St. Peter Port and bundled onto a boat that was built to carry only 200 passengers. It was a Dutch cargo ship, the Batavia, used for carrying cattle.

'The hours of waiting passed somehow and before dawn the children were going down to the harbour. I'm sure hardly anyone in Guernsey slept that night. Even people without children lay listening to the quick little footsteps passing their houses and the sleepy excited chatter.'

'We walked to a small balcony overlooking the harbour. We weren't allowed to go on the quayside to say goodbye. The day seemed like the longest we had ever lived through. We could hear the far off explosions on the French coast and we were afraid that the children wouldn't get away in time.

When the boat finally left, many hearts were heavy, we mothers had no idea where our children were going or if we would ever see them again. We were not to know that it would be almost 24 hours before they reached their destination. The ship arrived at Weymouth, where the children were given a meal, before boarding a train for the North.'

'It was the first time any of us had ever seen a train as there is no railway on Guernsey. Nobody knew what our destination was going to be. We asked the porter where we were going and he said "To Oldham, and God help you!".'

Right: David Hotton with his foster mum Mrs. Jessie Barker. Oldham 1940.

standards of behaviour; they showed me how to enjoy life to the full; they knew how to laugh. What a start in life I received. So you see I had a very good war. I was one of the lucky ones. I have a big soft spot for Lancashire.'

The children were allowed to send word home, via the Red Cross. The message had to contain no more than 25 words. The reply would be sent on the reverse & the same conditions applied. Meanwhile in Guernsey:

'The worry when we didn't hear from the children was awful. I used to cry myself to sleep every night. We felt completely cut off, it was nine months before we got the first Red Cross letter.'

'In Oldham I was taken in by the Hughes family. Mr. Hughes was a Methodist local preacher with two children of his own – John who was twelve years old and Ida – nine years old. I was settling in and getting to know the family when something happened which I have never been able to forget.

On 12th October 1941, which was Ida's tenth birthday, at around about midnight, the sirens sounded to herald an air raid mainly on Manchester, which was only five miles away. Although we had been told to get dressed, John and I were still in bed, when we heard a bomb screaming down and that was the last I knew for some time.

I came to, I don't know how long after, and found myself buried under debris. We had gone through the floor and I could feel the bricks, heavy masonry and flagstones from the pavement on top of me and smell the gas from the shattered mains. I can remember vividly praying earnestly as I lay

'As a little lad of six I was evacuated from Guernsey when it was threatened with invasion. I arrived at the home of Aunty Jessie and Uncle Fred Barker in Chapel Road, Hollinwood. They and their family poured out their love on me for four wonderful years. Although they were poor, we seemed to lack nothing. They saved up at the Bible Mission and they would take me to Fleetwood and the ferry, Blackpool and the big dipper, and many other places.'

'I believe that I owe a large measure of my happiness to my friends in Lancashire. They loved God; they loved me. They set me high

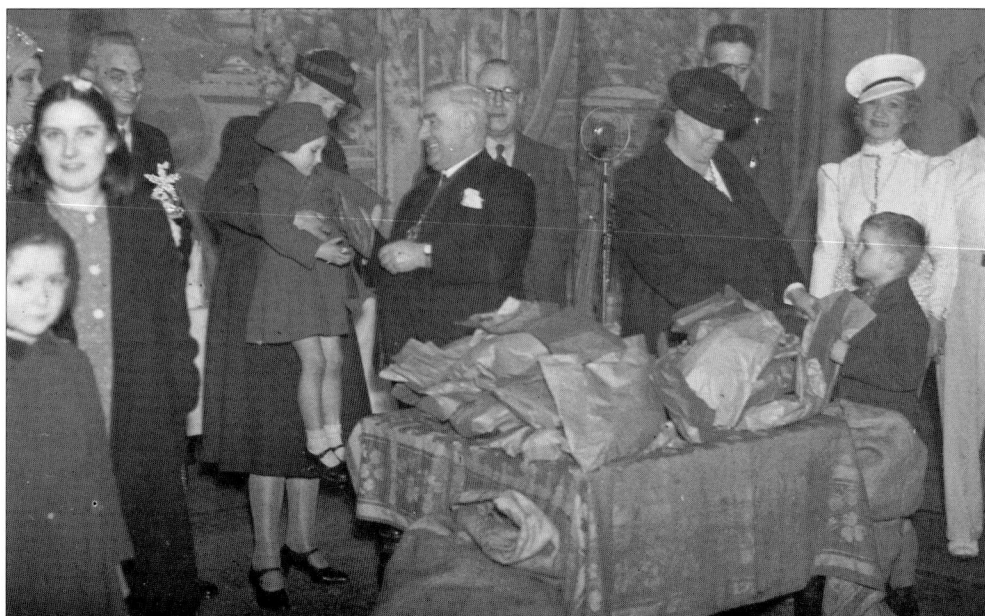

Left: Evacuees at the Empire Theatre to see Cinderella and collect a parcel. Organised by the W.V.S.

Opposite page: Red Cross Letters to David Hotton.

there waiting for help. I could move my hands slightly and clawed desperately to get out – to no avail. After what seemed like an eternity firemen dug me out, it was very slow, I was caked in mud and must have looked quite a shocked and forlorn sight sat there in my pyjamas. I was able to tell them that John was buried also. I learned much later that John and his mother had both been killed – just Mr. Hughes, Ida and myself had survived.'

The following piece was written in 1942 by one of the boys, while still in Oldham, probably so he would not forget.

I will now recount some of the things we have done and which have been made possible by the kindness of the Oldham people. We have been to four of the town's leading cinemas, The Gaumont, Odeon, Empire and Victory, and also to many of the football matches played at Oldham

Athletic's ground, Boundary Park. Indeed, one of our number, Sylvester K. Rabey, has played as a winger for "Latics". Others have been to the Rugby League Ground at Watersheddings, and many have also been weekly to the Public Baths, (Central and Chadderton). A novel experience was when thirty of us went down a coal-mine and saw all the life that goes on underground.

We are so happy in Oldham that when officials wanted to move us to Caernarvon, so loud were our protests that they decided to let us stay. Some of the boys later took part in a broadcast destined for transmission to the occupied Islands.

We can never thank the people of Oldham enough for all they have done for us. Here we are, for how long we do not know, but when we go back to our own dear Island eventually, please do not send us on the "Batavia IV".
Frederick J. Le Page.
June 3rd 1942.

Above: A war-time queue for nylons

At home

In 1941 when clothes rationing was introduced, it was difficult for anyone who became pregnant, because clothing coupons would not extend to maternity clothes and out came the old school gym slips to be altered accordingly. Army blankets were coveted for alteration into edge-to-edge coats. A bought maternity dress would have to be worn constantly and then would be lent out to other girls.

'I remember distinctly when my knickers wouldn't fit me any more, and I found two pairs of my husband's underpants, (he was stationed abroad at the time) and they were ideal. I must have looked a treat when I undressed at the doctor's, but it was better than none and I wanted my clothing coupons for other things.'

The most wonderful thing which was to happen to expectant mothers during the 2nd World War was the introduction of the 'green' ration book. It enabled them to obtain extra milk and although there was no legal obligation to give a pregnant woman priority, it became accepted that on showing the 'green' book, a pregnant woman could go to the front of the queue. News of scarce food items arriving at the shops quickly spread and when *very* occasionally oranges were delivered, a queue would soon form, the green ration book mothers or would-be mothers always were sure of getting their share.

'As a little girl I remember having to queue at Helingoes on Henshaw Street when onions had arrived, my Grandma was queueing at the Store for something else. People were only allowed one onion and that onion went into about five meat puddings. It must have been thrown in from the top of the stairs!'

Fashion had come to a standstill during the Second World War. Clothes rationing controlled spending and after 1941, every item of clothing bore the 'utility mark'. The general feeling was that with the return of peace, everything would immediately become more plentiful. Instead the end of the war resulted in queues becoming an integral part of the British way of life as practically everything was in short supply. The annual ration of clothing coupons which was 48 did not go very far. Shoes, if you could queue long enough – when a small supply came through, were nine coupons and a dress was 12. A mans suit in Utility cloth took 24, and a shirt seven coupons. If a couple were getting married, they could apply for a pair of cotton sheets, but it would cost them 39/11 (just short of £2) and 14 coupons. Relatives often came to the rescue with previous coupons.

'One of the worst things to go without, was silk stockings – unless you had an American boy-friend, they were virtually nil. We used to use leg-tan, which was like a brown dye and my mother used to go mad because it came off on the sheets. Some girls were really clever and drew a seam up the back.'

Extra clothing coupons could be obtained for children of a certain height and with large feet. Schools were responsible for measuring the children and this procedure made growing very desirable. Women let their hair grow long as implements like metal curling pins and kirby-grips disappeared from the shops.

'I remember my Dad going mad because I had used his pipe cleaners to curl my hair, you could wrap the hair round and bend the ends of the pipe cleaner to secure it – it was great. The hair could be kept tidy at work by cutting the top off a stocking to put round the head and tucking the hair into it. People called it the "Victory Roll".'

Turbans were seen everywhere, and girls could wear trousers without any derisive remarks for the first time ever! If it were possible to pin-point an obvious fashion, it has to be the first padded shoulders as clothes took on a military style, with fake epaulettes.

'During the war, a lot of girls got married before they knew anything about life. Because the boys were going away the girls were encouraged. I got married at eighteen and when my husband was away all my friends were having a good time. I was too young to be married obviously, and I resented it. I felt lost and trapped somehow, because I was married.'

'When I was 21 it was the 4th of July and from Ferrantis' we all went to a pub called Peveril of the Peak in Manchester. All these Yanks came in and of course they were celebrating Independence Day. When they realised it was my birthday they made a big fuss and I was on the piano playing Yankee songs. We got the last train from Manchester and when I walked in my Mother said, "Have you been drinking?" – "How do you know?" I said. My gasmask was round my neck, I must have looked a bit dishevelled, but we still talk about that night – me and my friends – the password was 'Keep in a crowd and you'll be safe".'

'One girl I remember, she became pregnant when her husband was away, she came in work and she was heartbroken. Some people at work condemned her and she went through hell. The attitudes were of course – patriotic – her husband was away

fighting for the country and she was looked upon as evil. Nobody would help her – she ended up having a back street abortion – it's a wonder she survived, but there was a lot of that then.'

'Me and my friend met these two boys in the blackout – it was really pitch you know – you could only hear voices sometimes and they took us in a milk bar on Yorkshire St – just to see what we looked like and I went out with one for a while – then I got fed up with him – I used to have lots of dates but you behaved. Some lads would say "don't be soft" – but we were frightened – I think we were always scared of the consequences, it made us behave.'

'In the blackout – the only way we could find our houses, when we had been to the pictures was – our step used to go in – in the middle. It was worn a bit – and you would feel with your foot and when my mother found ours – the other mothers would count from there. They'd shout – "Are you there Rosie?" Because quite a few neighbours would go to the pictures together, especially as most of the husbands were away at war.'

It actually became *legal* eventually to shine a torch as long as it was pointing downwards and there was some tissue paper over the glass – but No. 8 batteries were very scarce and when they arrived in the shops the queues were enormous. Early on in the blackout you could actually be fined for striking a match and having a lighted cigarette during an air-raid warning. People used to shout "put that light out!".

'When the sirens went, we all went into a pantry under the stairs. My Gran armed with her policies in a large handbag had got a kettle in the pantry and biscuits and comics etc. At first it was rather exciting and different, but after a bit I expect everybody got rather blasé, because we were only interested in what time it was when the "All Clear" sounded. If it went before midnight, we had to go to school the following morning, but if it went after midnight, we didn't go until lunchtime.'

'When the sirens went, we didn't go into the shelter in the yard – my mother didn't think it was adequate, it was only a square brick thing. We had a shelf in the living room, so we used to go under there and put the budgie under as

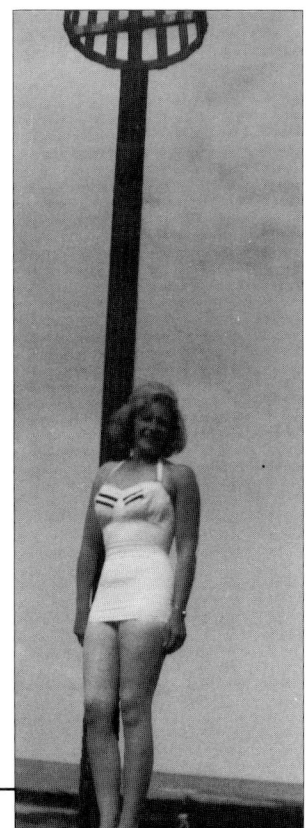

*Right: Hanging Ditch,
Manchester 23rd
December, 1940.*

*Below: Werneth Hall
Road, 12 October, 1941*

*Above left: Miller
Street, Manchester,
Christmas 1940.
Right: Bomb damage,
Manley Road.
Inset: Incline Road*

well. When we were at my Grandma's and the air-raid warning sounded – we had to go in Platt's shelter – there was a stage and people kept giving a turn and I did a bit of a tap dance.'

'I had woken up and heard this noise and rumbling and asked my mother what it was and she said it was thunder. The next thing, people were out in the street and we could hear someone shouting "Rosie, Rosie, wake up" and it was the flying bomb which hit Abbeyhills.'

'We were all in the shelter, the sirens had gone and the door of the shelter faced the house. Quite suddenly, we could see the house all lit up – the German plane had dropped flares – perhaps so they could see their target. I think they were aiming for the "shadow factory" (now Seddons) which was engaged in war work. Next, we heard the bomb come whistling down and everyone in the shelter

was totally silent . . . we were just waiting – it could be us – we didn't know – then we heard this terrific bang and we knew it had hit something. The "shadow factory" had only had the one incendiary on the roof – which the fire-fighters put out – but in Turf Lane the factory there had gone, it was just wiped out – it was a pile of rubble.'

'I remember vividly one of the nights they bombed Manchester and I went up to the top of the "rope walk" steps, (named because of its close proximity to Oldham Rope and Twine works) and you saw Manchester blazing – you could actually see the bombing, and buildings bursting into flames. It brought it home to me when I went afterwards with my brother for plumbing equipment and Baxendales – which was a vast warehouse, covering a huge area. It had gone – just wiped out. Of course Oldham was so near to Manchester.'

'We lived in Alt Lane and I remember one night when friends came to our house and their little girl was put in my bed. I awoke in the night to this most peculiar noise – I had never heard anything like it before. It was a flying bomb, but I didn't know at the time. I grabbed this little girl, Judith she was called and ran into my Mum and Dad's room and we all went into the Morrison shelter in the dining room. We had first aid and food always in there. The parents of Judith had gone home, they must have been worried sick, because they borrowed a bike and finally got to us and were so happy and relieved to find us alive.'

Oldham "Holidays at Home"

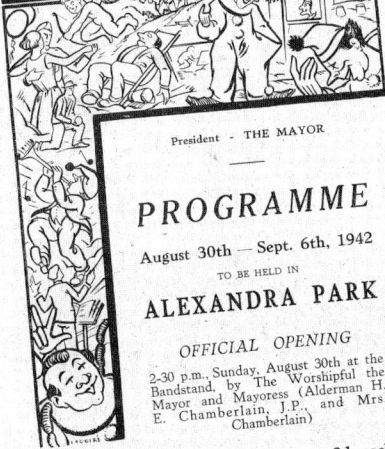

YOUTH ON PARADE

Produced by M. H. Taylor.
Lyrics and Libretto, Tom Green.

When it was considered unsafe to travel because of air-raids, many Northern towns organised "Holidays at Home". Oldham's Wakes celebrations were always in Alexandra Park with dancing to a band and if young men were home on leave – the activities were an added bonus.

County Borough of Oldham

HOLIDAYS AT HOME

President - THE MAYOR

PROGRAMME

August 30th — Sept. 6th, 1942

TO BE HELD IN

ALEXANDRA PARK

OFFICIAL OPENING

2-30 p.m. Sunday, August 30th at the Bandstand, by The Worshipful the Mayor and Mayoress (Alderman H. E. Chamberlain, J.P., and Mrs. Chamberlain)

Programme - - - 2d. each

Always carry your Programme with you. Prizes will be distributed each day at various centres to those who can produce a programme on demand

TIMES PRINTING CO.,
UNION ST., OLDHAM.

'I remember when I was a little girl, Mr Lieboldt. He had a jeweller's shop on Henshaw St and was a clock-maker. At one time during the war people gathered round his shop, I believe there was about five hundred. He must have been really frightened. It was because he was German, he had already lost one of his boys in the first world war. Anyway I believe he eventually committed suicide.'

THURSDAY, 3rd SEPTEMBER

2-30 p.m.

OPENING OF THE
R.A.F. EXHIBITION
at the ART GALLERY, UNION STREET.
by The Worshipful The Mayor.
Accompanied by Air Commodore J. G. Murray.

The Guard of Honour will be inspected in front of the Town Hall at 2 p.m. by the Mayor and the Air Commodore and will afterwards proceed to Alexandra Park by way of Yorkshire Street, Rhodes Bank, Union Street, King Street, Park Road.

Open Daily from 10 a.m. to 8 p.m. until September 19th.

BAND PERFORMANCE, ALEXANDRA PARK
THE ROYAL AIR FORCE BAND
(by kind permission of the Group Captain Commanding).

CONCERTS ON THE PROMENADE
THE "NINE-TWO-FIVERS"
ROYAL AIR FORCE CONCERT PARTY
(by permission of the Group Captain Commanding).

7-30 p.m.

C.E.M.A. CONCERT
TOWN HALL
Chairman: The Mayor Elect (Ald. T. Driver, J.P.).
ARTISTES:
DALE SMITH, Baritone.
DORA GILSON, Pianist.
HENRY HOLST, Violinist.
ADMISSION FREE.
Silver Collection.

6-30 p.m.

MILITARY SWIMMING GALA
CENTRAL BATHS.
Chairman: The Deputy Mayor (Coun. W. H. Taylor).
Commencing 6-30 p.m.
Events:

1. One Length Free Style.
2. Two Lengths Back Stroke.
3. Three Lengths Breast Stroke.
4. Six Lengths Free Style.
5. Plain Dive (3 Heights).
6. Plunge
7. Medley Team Race.
8. Team Race.
9. Obstacle Race.
10. Water Polo Match.

Admission 6d.

AMBULANCE TENT, LOST CHILDREN'S TENT and LOST PROPERTY TENT at Alexandra Park.
AIR RAID SHELTERS at Park Square Entrance, Alexandra Road Schools and adjoining Games Ground.

FRIDAY, 4th SEPTEMBER

2-30 p.m.

NATIONAL FIRE SERVIC
KINGS ROAD

Squad Marching.
Erection of 5,000 Gallon Scaffold Dam.
Pump Competition.
Pump Drill Display by Fire Women.
Turntable Escape
Foam Display.
Massed Jet Displa
Demonstration of External Water

Commentator: Column Officer Walkden.
The Committee express their thanks to F. Dar Commander, for his kind permission in allowing t and to Divisional Officer B. Bellamy and to all have given their services.

2-30 p.m.

BAND PERFORMANCE.
THE BAND of the 12th CENTRE PIO
(by kind permission of Lt.-Col. H. Greenwood, V

6-0 p.m.

OLDHAM CIVIL DEFENCE C
(by kind permission of the Controller, W. E.

2-30 p.m. and 6-0 p.m.

CONCERTS ON THE PROMENAD
12th CENTRE PIONEER CORPS CONC
(by kind permission of Lt.-Col. H. Greenwood, V

7-0 p.m. to 11 p.m.

HOLIDAY DAN
HILL STORES, GREENACRES
7 to 11 p.m.
Band: 12th Centre Pioneer Corps Broad Orchestra.
Admission 3/-.
Tickets on sale at Electricity Showrooms, Union Showrooms, Market Place, or from Members of the N.A.L.G.O.
Refreshments obtainable at reasonable charges.

SATURDAY, 5th SEPTEMBER

2-30 p.m. and 6-0 p.m.

BAND PERFORMANCE
The Band of The Manchester R
(by kind permission of the Officer Comman
DIRECTOR OF MUSIC: L. STATH

3-0 p.m. and 6-0 p.m.

CONCERT ON THE PROMENAD
12th CENTRE PIONEER CORPS CONCER

7-0 p.m.

PRESENTATION OF PRIZ
AT THE BANDSTAND
By THE WORSHIPFUL THE MAYOR (Ald. H. E. Cha
Chairman: Alderman R. Roberts, J.P.

DON'T FORGET, IF YOU WANT TEA BRING YOUR

During the Second World War, a task that many people enjoyed and found worthwhile was collecting 'salvage'. The system of hoarding things with the idea that they might come in useful someday was suddenly shattered when people realised the 'sometime' had arrived.

In July 1940, the W.V.S. appealed to the people of Britain for anything made of aluminium which could be melted down to help towards making a Spitfire. Old pans and other cooking utensils of every kind were taken to a collecting depot, and by the time the aluminium appeal ended 2 months later, it had yielded a thousand tons of metal.

As the war progressed other salvage collections were organised and local Guides and Scouts helped the W.V.S. in this. Carrier bags would be hung on door knockers and when collected a couple of hours later would certainly be full. National advertisements were put up everywhere, encouraging people to collect everything from milk bottle tops, old envelopes, jam jars and even bones. In many residential areas large boxes and bins appeared labelled 'metal', 'paper', 'bone', pig bin etc.

In February 1942 Picture Post decided to encourage the salvage drive by asking people to save paper and magazines by printing the following:
The war is driving Hitler back
And here's one way to win it
Just give your salvage men the sack
And see there's plenty in it.

By 1943, libraries everywhere were involved and there was the largest clear-out of books in British history as the campaign yielded 56 million volumes in six months.

'Every couple of days, somebody would move the 'pig-bin'. In warm weather it smelled awful and, of course, nobody wanted it outside their house.'

'When you went to do your 'buying in' at the store, there was a large notice behind the counter, saying "Use the number 50 and give it to Joe". As a little girl I used to think Joe was the man who owned the Co-op. Later I found out it was Joe Stalin.'

'One Saturday afternoon, my Mum took us both to the Palladium cinema on Union Street. She hadn't heard from my Dad for quite a few weeks – but of course we didn't know that. We were near the front, about half way and a notice came on the screen "Will Mrs. Alice Gee go to the foyer immediately." My Mum said to me and Mona "Don't move, stay there!", then my Mum went to the foyer, but of course we kept looking round and then we shouted out "It's me Dad!" We shot up and ran – everyone in the cinema knew – they were all so happy for us – nobody was watching the picture – real life was more important. When I got to him, the first thing I said was, "What have you brought me?" My Mum was cross with me about that afterwards, but we were only kids.'

' "Goodnight children – everywhere"
Those final words by Uncle Mac made you feel as if everything was alright, even though there was a war on. I think the sentence that provoked the most fear in my heart was at the end of the news, sometimes the reader would say "and one of our aircraft is missing" I hated him saying that and I was only a little girl, so you see, children were affected by the news.'

'We had a big salvage drive at school, when we all promised to bring at least one carrier bag full and as many comics and paper that we could carry.'

"Goodnight children everywhere"

Left: German Prisoners of War in Crete Street, August 1945.

Prisoners

In 1943 many German prisoners were brought to Oldham & the Glen Mill was taken over as a prisoner of war camp.

'I was fighting against the New Zealand soldiers and then I came back to Holland and I was captured there by Canadian soldiers, and this was very hard for me because I had just been married three weeks before and I don't know what happens and if I see my wife again and my parents, and everybody. We were taken to England by ship, about three or four hundred, it was a warship and I was terribly sea-sick.'

'After a time in Sheffield, then Bury, I came to Oldham. It was the camp number 166 and my first meeting with Edith and Jack.
It was Christmas time and they were asked to invite a prisoner of war to their home and this was a very good feeling for me – it has been the best impression of my life. It was a very good thing for our countries. I could not write to my wife at this time and it wasn't until 1946 I got the first letter from my wife through the Red Cross. I must say that I met very nice people here in England – they show me much kindness and I not forget and sometime when people come to my town now, people say to them "go to Otto Adler, he is the Englishman in Germany!".'

'It had been an old cotton mill – the camp. It was a high place with seven storeys and I was working in the clothing store – it was in the shelter – no sunshine there, but in the evening time I was able to go out and work on a farm about two kilometres away, and working hay-making. This was very interesting for me, because I am a farmer too and the local farmer had about six cows

and I said I had not done milking and he say to me 'that's not possible – you are a farmer and no milking?" when I go back to the Glen Mill – there are about 2,000 prisoners of war by then. It is very full of men and the Oldham people, they look at us when they are walking past the Glen Mill and I think they are saying "they are very hard Nazis", but not many have been Nazis and all the prisoners of war, who had been a Nazi before, changed their mind at this time. In Germany, in Hitler time, he has been a dictator – he say what you do and everything has been exactly done and in England it is quite different and I think the English prison has been a very good lesson and school for their lives afterwards in Germany.'

'It was only a three mile radius when we were allowed out of the camp, but Edith's father had a car and he said we would go to Blackpool. Mr Shaw gave me some clothes to change into – civilian clothes, so nobody could find out that I am a German prisoner. It was a nice time, because for the first time in Blackpool I see the sea, I see the lake at home in Germany, but not the sea.'

Below: Glen Mill, where the prisoners of war lived for a number of years.

'When we went out to the farm or anywhere – we had a British soldier for escort and these men some of them have had plenty of experience and seen danger. He gave me the gun to carry back to the camp, he didn't bother anymore. Eventually we were able to go out without escort to visit friends we had made. I came home to South Germany and it had been the first meeting with my wife for four and half years.'

Left: Fritz Kamm and Eric Duwe – Two prisoners of war at the Glen Mill. While employed haymaking they heard that the local tennis club had no caretaker and offered to take on the job, Fritz having been a qualified tennis coach in Berlin. Arising from this, deep and lasting friendships were formed between families.

Above: Re-united,Otto and Inge, outside their home 'Brielhof'. 1949.

Prisoners of war clearing the snow from the rugby ground at Watersheddings in preparation for the match against Leigh. Jan. 31st 1947.

Prisoners of war at the Glen Mill in 1947 – two years after the war was over and still waiting to go home.

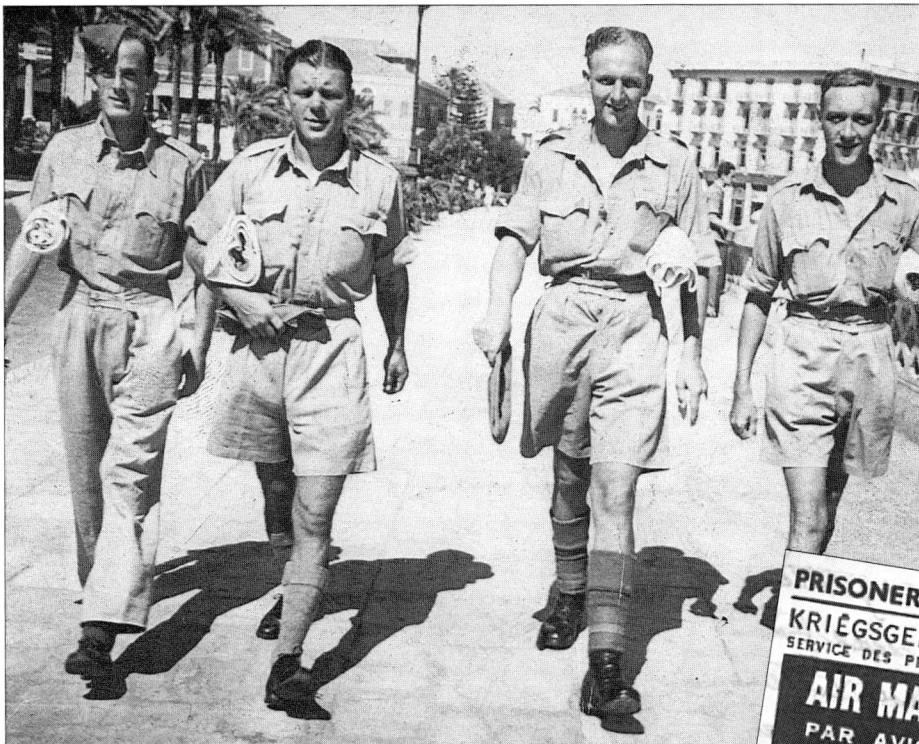

*On a weeks leave in Beirut,
the first for 4½ years.*

*Air Mail letter Returned from
continent in undelivered mail.*

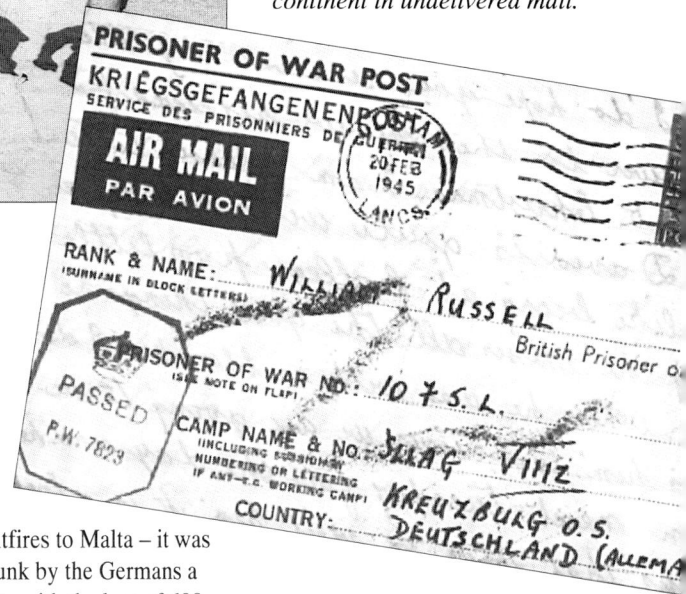

They went away

*Time, like an ever-rolling stream,
Bears all its sons away;
They fly forgotten as a dream
Dies at the opening day.*

Isaac Watts

'It was 1940 and I wanted to join the R.A.F., but when I went to volunteer it was New Year's Day and they were closed. Imagine a war on and they were shut!'

'I went down the day after and got my King's shilling for joining. Me and my mate had both decided we would volunteer, but his girlfriend cried and didn't want him to go ... and he never went.'

'I was only in 10 days when I was sent to France. There were 12 men in our Sub-section, four married, four engaged and four with girl friends and at the end of the war only one finished up with his girl.'

'At first I got 25/– a week, plus 7/– a week stopped from Jack's pay to keep me and the two little ones. It was a real struggle and used to make me really mad when I knew what some were getting on munitions. Jack was left with 1/– a day after my allowance was out – that was for leaving his family and risking his life! After a while, I think some M.P. fought for a rise for us and we got about £3 a week, but I'm sure it wasn't until nearly the end of the war.'

'In 1942 I went off on a course to become a Gunner instructor and during this time the

Eagle was carrying Spitfires to Malta – it was loaded up, but it was sunk by the Germans a couple of days off Malta with the loss of 600 lives. Wherever there was an aircraft carrier there was always an attendant destroyer ready for anything going wrong and it picked a survivor up who was a mate of mine. My name musn't have been on that one!'

*Harry Kelsall, (in tank)
before El Alamein.*

'Eagle – showing tail of aeroplane coming in to land. If one crashed onto the deck, it would burst into flames – there was never any hesitation – we would all shove it over the side into the water and the crew would jump out!'

Ralph Mellor c 1941

'When I got my calling up papers my mother was very upset – she had been a widow for 12 years and I was her only son!'
'When we eventually got to Calcutta we were allowed to send a telegram home – I thought how thrilled my Mother would be to receive it.

We were trekking through this wood when we got ambushed. We were about what they called "Milestone Log" – on the borders of India and Burma. We dived in a hollow and I had a radio and the other unit was brought up under cover of darkness.

We pushed our way through Elephant grass with some trepidation. Many skirmishes took place and some men were wounded or killed. On one occasion we came under attack from the Japanese mortars. As we grovelled amid the exploding shells I heard Taffy say "God, I've been hit!" The terrible burning sensation was in his upper arm. I rolled over and gingerly felt my way up his arm and took out of his sleeve a piece of shrapnel, it was extremely hot. We were both lucky.'

'Ralph was a wireless man and many was the time I was with him listening to the News and he was writing it down as fast as it was spoken in longhand. He had a speed system all his own. We had many a shock when we were lying quietly – we would hear the news in English from Japan telling the world that the victorious Jap Army had annihilated our Division.'

'While we were attempting to blow up the U.S. aircraft to prevent the Japanese using it, we thought at that moment that the Japs were right up country – we didn't realise they were right on our doorstep. We hadn't even started blowing them up when we were invaded. Some of us managed to get away – we jumped on this lorry. We didn't know where we were going – we just kept going and arrived at a place called Vandong in Java. When we got to this place, everything was going on as normal – we drew up in this main street and people were going to the cinema and the Japs were only about 30 miles way which is nothing in a war – it was just like a normal Sunday afternoon, we couldn't believe it.

They put us in a camp which was a Javanese camp and a funny incident was – we saw this brand new cinema and one of the lads said "We'll go there tonight" so we went over the wall – we had no pledge anyway, because we were on the Western desert to begin with. Anyhow, the following day, we were all filing past and the Japs had been over early that morning and the cinema was flat. I turned to Frank and said "Eh, look at that, we were in there last night." He said "I'm not surprised, it were a bloody awful picture anyway!".'

'We went in the hills – we had our orders to make for the coast and there would probably be ships to take us off – but when we got there, it was like Oldham Park Boating Lake on Christmas Day – nothing floating at all. We couldn't go any further, so we were taken prisoner then. We were caught with our backs to the wall.'

When we were captured – we thought we'd had it – they were very arrogant. They all had big swords trailing behind them and kept pushing us around. Afterwards they took us to this tea plantation and this prison. They banged the door and made a big issue out of locking it. It's a terrible feeling being locked in a cell. They pushed some rice under the door to us and we pushed it back, but eventually we were glad of it.

Changi was so overcrowded and it was so hot we couldn't breathe. We didn't wear trousers or a uniform – only a G-string – there was so much illness and men died, there was all sorts of diseases. If anybody retaliated it was terrible. I saw one officer who did and they broke his wrists. We were taken to this place to dig tunnels in the hillside, well we had no idea – but we used to dig two metres before we did any supporting. They would dip the logs in creosote and put them on our shoulders and they were so hot – but you couldn't take them off – they were so slippery – you couldn't have picked them up again – many men were buried – but life was cheap, so they never bothered.

When the Japanese came into the cell, we had to bow and every time we encountered a Japanese soldier we had to bow. After a few years, it isn't surprising that it became a habit that was still with me when I returned home and I was bowing every time anyone appeared.

I got home in October 1945. The Ghurkas came and took over the Japanese guards and eventually , we were free. It was a Saturday afternoon and all the family were at our house. Our Alice said "We've done your favourite sweet – rice pudding!" – what a joke!'

And when the strife is fierce, the warfare long, Steals on the ear the distant triumph song, And hearts are brave again, and arms are strong.

William W. How

Left: Allied prisoners in the notorious Changi Gaol, into which the Japanese herded thousands of troops. The photograph shows them just after the hour of liberation, weak but happy.

レンゴウグンノホリョヘ

ALLIED PRISONERS

The JAPANESE Government has surrendered. You will be evacuated by ALLIED NATIONS forces as soon as possible.

Until that time your present supplies will be augmented by air-drop of U.S. food, clothing and medicines. The first drop of these items will arrive within one (1) or two (2) hours.

Clothing will be dropped in standard packs for units of 50 or 500 men. Bundle markings, contents and allowances per man are as follows:

BUNDLE MARKINGS

CONTENTS	ALLOWANCES PER MAN	50 MAN PACK	500 MAN PACK	CONTENTS	ALLOWANCES PER MAN
Drawers	2	B	10	Laces, shoe	1
Undershirt	2	A	11	Kit, sewing	1
Socks (pr)	2	C	31	Soap, toilet	1
Shirt	1	C	4-6	Razor	1
Trousers	1	C	4-6	Blades, razor	10
Jacket, field	1	C	10	Brush, tooth	1
, web, waist	1	B	31	Paste, tooth	1
H.B.T.	1	C	10	Comb	1
(pr)	1	B	32	Shaving cream	1
Handkerchiefs	3	C	12-21	Powder(insecticide)	1
	1				

...tructions with the food and medicine for their use and distri-

CAUTION

MEDICATE   FOLLOW DIRECTIONS

INSTRUCTIONS FOR FEEDING 100 MEN

the first three (3) days, the following blocks (individual assembled:

1 Block No. 5
(Each Contains)

1 Case Soup, Dehd
1 Case Veg Puree
1 Case Bouillon
1 Case Hosp Supplies
1 Case Vitamin Tablets

1 Block No. 3
(Each Contains)

1 Case Candy
1 Case Gum
1 Case Cigarettes
1 Case Matches

1 Block No. 7
(Each Contains)

1 Case Nescafe
1 Sack Sugar
1 Case Milk
1 Case Cocoa

1 Block No. 10
(Each Contains)

3 Cases Fruit
2 Cases Juice

BUCKINGHAM PALACE

The Queen and I bid you a very warm welcome home.

Through all the great trials and sufferings which you have undergone at the hands of the Japanese, you and your comrades have been constantly in our thoughts. We know from the accounts we have already received how heavy those sufferings have been. We know also that these have been endured by you with the highest courage.

We mourn with you the deaths of so many of your gallant comrades.

With all our hearts, we hope that your return from captivity will bring you and your families a full measure of happiness, which you may long enjoy together.

George R.I.

'They shall not grow old as we
that are left grow old,
Age shall not weary them, nor
the years condemn,
At the going down of the sun and
in the morning, we will
remember them.'
Laurence Binyon

*Right: Ronald Scholes –
missing 1942, aged 19.*

*Below: The funeral cermony of
the sailors from H.M. Charybdis
and H.M. Limbourne at St. Peter
Port Guernsey*

When the H.M.S. Charybdis was sunk in the English Channel some of the bodies were washed ashore on Guernsey and some reached the shores of France and were secretly buried by French civilians who were not in a position to report their actions. Later, when France was liberated, many of the bodies were exhumed and reburied by the Imperial War Graves Commission in St. Brieuc Cemetery in France. It was more than six long years, before Ronald Scholes' mother was able to establish what had happened to her son and she would be one of many mothers who suffered this torment.

'My mother never gave in about Ronald until she received this letter. She knew of course about the ship going down, and wrote to everyone who might know anything … who might have seen what happened and she did get one letter from a friend of Ronalds', saying the last time he saw Ronald, he was in the water. This news gave her some hope, because she knew that he was a powerful swimmer and being a mother of course she didn't want to ever face losing him – he was only nineteen.'

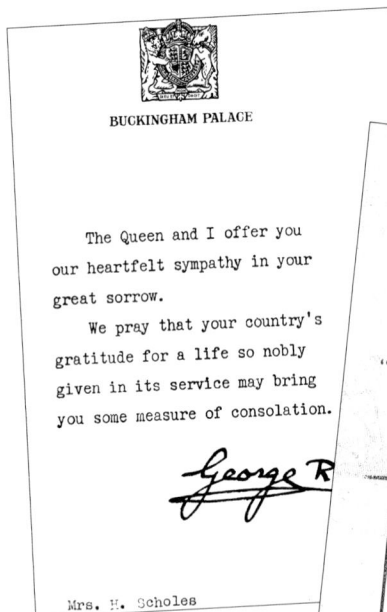

BUCKINGHAM PALACE

The Queen and I offer you
our heartfelt sympathy in your
great sorrow.

We pray that your country's
gratitude for a life so nobly
given in its service may bring
you some measure of consolation.

George R

Mrs. H. Scholes

Letter from the War Office.

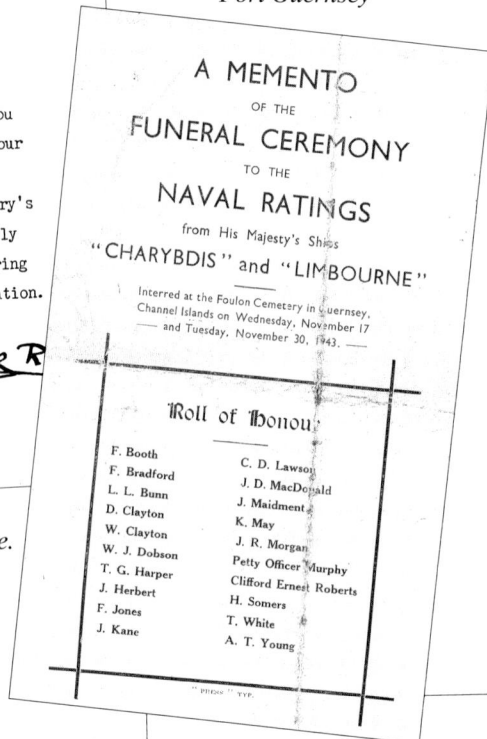

A MEMENTO
OF THE
FUNERAL CEREMONY
TO THE
NAVAL RATINGS
from His Majesty's Ships
"CHARYBDIS" and "LIMBOURNE"

Interred at the Foulon Cemetery in Guernsey,
Channel Islands on Wednesday, November 17
and Tuesday, November 30, 1943.

Roll of Honour

F. Booth	C. D. Lawson
F. Bradford	J. D. MacDonald
L. L. Bunn	J. Maidment
D. Clayton	K. May
W. Clayton	J. R. Morgan
W. J. Dobson	Petty Officer Murphy
T. G. Harper	Clifford Ernest Roberts
J. Herbert	H. Somers
F. Jones	T. White
J. Kane	A. T. Young

*Below: Boys Brigade Membership
Card 1944-45. The mother of Ronald
Scholes continued to receive these
from the Boy's Brigade, many years
after the war, when it was known that
Ronald had perished as the ship he
served on was sunk by German E –
boats in the English Channel in
October 1942.*

Pause a sigh
Over the mounds of fresh-turned
earth where lie
Those mariners asleep
Softly weep
For their loved ones across the deep
Who wait for them in vain;
Theirs the pain
Of watching for a ship to come again
Which nevermore will sail:
Worn and pale
The sweethearts, wives and mothers
of the crew
Who courted death and knew
Sweet adieu.
Mavis Mallett

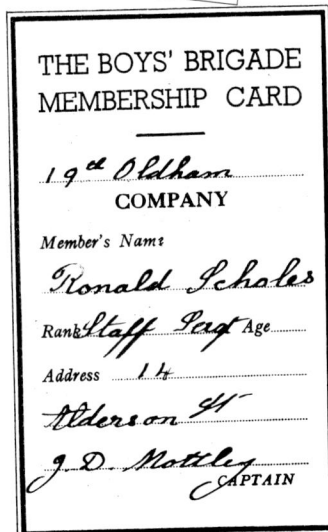

THE BOYS' BRIGADE MEMBERSHIP CARD

19th Oldham
COMPANY

Member's Name *Ronald Scholes*

Rank *Staff Sergt* Age

Address *14*

Alderson St

J. D. Nottley
CAPTAIN

THE BOYS' BRIGADE

The Object of the Brigade is the advancement of Christ's Kingdom among Boys, and the promotion of habits of Obedience, Reverence, Discipline, Self-Respect, and all that tends towards a true Christian Manliness.

The Boys' Brigade was founded in 1883 by Sir William A. Smith. The total strength to-day exceeds 100,000 Officers and Boys. Boys of the Brigade are expected to do their utmost to maintain its good name and high traditions.

Boys over 12 years of age are eligible for enrolment, and may remain members until the age of liability for military service.

A prize is offered to Staff-Sergeants or Boys of the Brigade for the best design for the Card for Session 1945-46. Designs should be sent to the Brigade Offices, through Captains of Companies, not later than 1st March, 1945.

V.E. day celebration, Kenwood Rd., 1945 'The community spirit was wonderful when our children were small.'

Below: Bonfire at Grasscroft. V.J. Day. August 15th 1945.

1945

V.E. Day – Albert Mount, Derker. Dr. Struthers and family. Borrowed the form from the Methodist Chapel.

There were crowds outside the Town Hall and all sat on the steps. People were singing and the pubs around were doing a roaring trade. Tomorrow the parties would begin . . . . Oldham, like other Northern towns, had a lot of practice in the elusive art of street parties, with the Jubilee in 1935, Edward the VIII in 1936, and George VI Coronation in 1937, but this one was different. It was more than a celebration, it was a turning point from the fear of life being as short as a shoe-lace to a future to look forward to.

Everyone knew everyone and because most of the streets were narrow, the tables stretched right across the street. The war years had demanded a strength and tolerance from women which was almost superhuman and as always they had responded with humour and love . . . today they had something to sing about.

'Someone brought out this gramophone – we had turns at winding it up. We could stay up until dark, it must have been midnight, everyone was dancing it was lovely. We sang "When the lights go on again, all over the world" and then we did the okey, kokey and the conga right through Mr Ashworth's garden – well he would never have tolerated that any other time! All in all, it was a sight never to be forgotten.'

19 May 1945 the Board of Trade issued a statement:

'Until the end of May you may buy cotton bunting without coupons, as long as it is red, white or blue and does not cost more than 1/3 a square yard.'

'My dad came home on V.E. day – the 8th May 1945 and at the time we were at a street party in the next street, which was Thorn Street. A little lad came and told us, then everybody crowded into our house. He hadn't seen us for four years and of course the biggest change was in me, because I was 15 when he came home and I felt quite strange with him at first.'

'Trestle tables were borrowed from Sunday School – we used large planks of wood for tables – somebody, I remember took their lavatory door off. I'm not sure which party that was for. They were covered with white sheets and out from all the neighbouring houses came mountains of sandwiches, quivering jelly and any available seating, old chairs, forms from Sunday School, and the chippy. We drank cream soda and some Tizer, and of course there was gallons of tea served from teapots that could have been used for giants.'

The exile is at home:
O nights and days of tears!
O longings not to roam,
O sins, and doubts, and fears.
What matters now grief's
    darkest day,
Peace has wiped those tears
    away.

'The British people had risen, without fuss, to unparalleled heights of sacrifice and resolution. They deserved a reward.'
Historian A.J.P. Taylor, at the end of the war and peace in Europe.

BRAVE NEW WORLD

Growing up

. . .that time is past,
And all its' aching joys are now
no more
And all its dizzy raptures. Not
for this
Faint I, nor mourn, nor
murmer, other gifts
Have followed: for such loss, I
would believe,
Abundant recompense. For I
have learned
To look on nature, Not as in the
hour
Of thoughtless youth, but
hearing oftentimes
The still, sad music of
humanity.

W. Wordsworth

The things you remember about growing up are very different from today, because nothing was related to television. The most glamorous people in both male and female adolescents lives were film-stars. Records were 78's and it was something special to have a record player which played L.P.'s. Tangee Lipstick, Yardley's English Rose, Californian Poppy, Miners Lip-Line, Brylcreem, Max Factor's Pancake and Pasha Cigarettes were all passports to a heaven so tender, so alluring, and birth pangs of a brave new world.'

.After the 2nd World War, adaptation and change became key factors. For the first time for many years, worker's interests and needs were taken into account by many employers when considering measures to increase productivity. A new word constantly used was 'automaton', in reference to machines which would displace human labour. There was much talk of the advantages to the consumer and of price reduction by these methods.

Rapid technology changes such as redundancy, the need for re-deployment and re-training were subjects not yet thought of. For the Oldham populance, life was fun again, air-raids had finished, the blackout curtains could go and although rationing was to continue for some time, items were slowly returning to the shops.

'I announced in the Check office at the Co-op, "they've got Yardleys in the chemist!" and it was if I'd shouted "fire!" All the girls ran out with their handbags and began queueing until supplies had finished.'

'I wrote to a boy stationed in Gibraltar who could get nylon stockings and we would ask him to send them for us – any size it didn't matter. They were a vile colour – bright tan, but it was an improvement on leg tan, at least they had a seam.'

The 1950s saw the appearance of the first boutiques, they were less formal than the usual department stores and created a classless fashion that had never before appeared.

'Sunday afternoon, after Sunday School we used to go in the park (Alexandra) – everyone did. We would all be dressed in our Sunday best – then we didn't wear Sunday clothes through the week . . . so everybody used to pose about. You would see what the boys looked like in daylight. Some of them would sit on the forms of the long walk and eye the girls up as they passed. It was good fun, the refreshment room at the top of the steps was always crowded.'

Like Phoenix from the ashes, Dior's New Look burst upon Oldham c 1948. It brought back femininity to a post war world, making Dior's name as well known as that of Churchill. It required a small waist and lots of fullness in the skirt. It brought with it padded bras and 'shaped to figure' jackets.

'I was going to the art school at the time studying fashion design and because of this I was a bit more adventurous. I bought this coat from Jones' in Manchester. It had an eight gore skirt starting at the hips, very heavy, all wool – pale blue and brown herringbone with a brown velvet collar and I wore it with brown suede shoes and a brown velvet hat. Walking down the long walk in Oldham Park, I thought I was the bees knees, it was the absolute to me – fashion personified – what a poser!'

'You had to go to the Co-op first – King St. store in my case. If they hadn't got what you were looking for – then you could try somewhere else. Morris's shoe shop was our mecca – everybody went there. It was in the arcade and on Saturdays it was crowded. It was there we discovered the first stilettos – the pointed Italian toes, the very first coloured leather shoes 5 inch heels you could hardly walk in.'

'I had bought these high heels and I was trying them out for the night holding onto the wall behind the house – really struggling, when my father was coming home, round the corner. "What the hell are you doing in those bloody daft shoes?" he said "You are going to break your neck!" I knew that I wanted to wear them for dancing that night and I was determined. I managed it eventually, they crippled me, but I danced in them all night.'

'In the 50's 'see- through nighties' were new and daring and I went to Grafton House with my friend who bought one for her honeymoon. She had to hide it when she got home, she daren't have shown it her mother. Even the woman in the shop said it would be alright with her vest underneath!'

Above: Mollie Sykes, Barbara Sykes, Joan Whitehead and Joan Burridge, showing off Marks and Spencers fashions in Alexandra Park c1948.

Below: Lesley Jones, age 15 sat on the garden wall at Horsedge Street wearing the height of fashion, bouffant skirt and shoes from Morris's in the Arcade.

Above: Lesley Jones wearing whispies and drainpipes.

Right: Marjorie Gee and Doreen Kemp in Gordonia bras!

Below: Isle of Man 1954

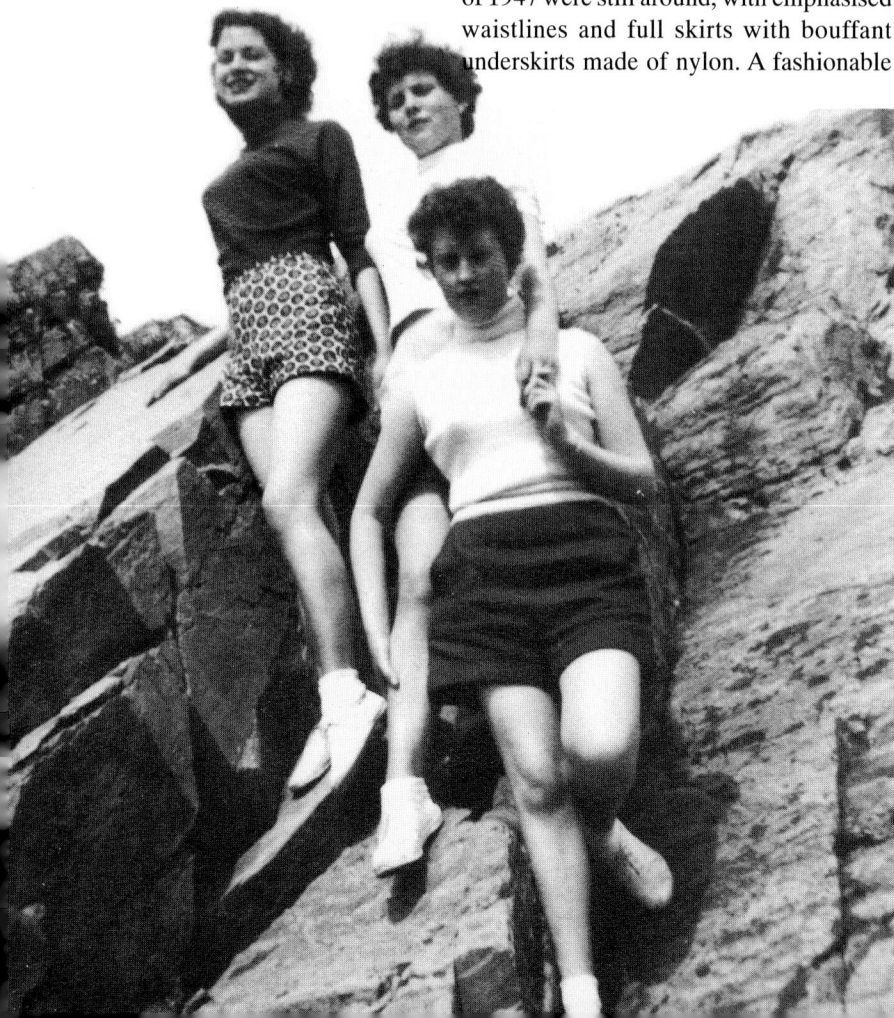

When the word teenager arrived from America, it brought with it many new ideas. For the first time ever, young people had their own fashions. Previous to this, girls especially, dressed exactly like their Mothers. Designers took the opportunity of catering for these new wage earners and consequently bewildered them and fashion became erratic.

In the 50's, shadows of the 'New Look' of 1947 were still around, with emphasised waistlines and full skirts with bouffant underskirts made of nylon. A fashionable girl would be hatted and gloved, even in summer without coat. In contrast, toreador trousers appeared and were worn by the new 'teenager' with a cardigan buttoned up the back, huge plastic earrings, ballerina shoes and a pony tail.

'These Gordonia bras they were circular stitched with very fine tape sewn inside and conical shape like Madonna wears now. They were from Grafton House on Yorkshire St. I went upstairs and tried it with my jumper over the top, because I couldn't wait to go out in it. When I came downstairs again, my father said, "Christ, tha's bin in't pencil sharpener!" Everybody had a Gordonia bra – it was the thing. If anybody leaned against you the bras would cave in, they were so stiff.'

In your teens, the need not to be solitary, but to be part of a group encouraged a self-conscious behaviour. There was very little individuality, most young people if they admitted it were nervous of experiment. It was a rather silly, almost defiant, but enjoyable existence.

'We decided one night to make these face-packs. We used Rinso and Fuller's Earth cream and when it dried on our faces, we daren't look at each other – it had set like steel! It is a wonder we didn't do ourselves damage. Well I started laughing, I was in hysterics and mine cracked, of course I was convinced that I had ruined my beauty treatment. If someone had knocked on the door, I think we would have had to hide.'

'It's all mine!' Terry Conn's 21st Birthday

'We used to use these curling tongs, heat them up in a fire and put them in front of your hair – you had to have a Tony Curtis hair cut of course and then you'd just curl this front bit. Coming home from holiday once we'd all packed our cases and the woman came in – probably to make sure we hadn't left the room in a mess and she shouted, "Eh, you've forgotten these" and held up these curling tongs. It was embarrassing – you weren't supposed to do anything like that in those days – they would say you were 'sissys'. In the 50's, it was girls-there and boys-there and never the twain shall meet. Girls were pretty little things, taffeta skirts, stiletto heels etc.'

The 1950's were a time of recovery and discovery. Years of rationing were over and a population of young people who had their sights set on marriage reached out eagerly to a promising future. Material was plentiful once more and everyone took advantage of this. Many brides wore 'ballerina' length dresses, still influenced by the 'New Look' of the late 40's.

'I had these shoes called 'Bare necessities.' I think Clarks made them and that's all they were – just a few thin straps and I wore them with a hobble skirt that I couldn't stride out in. I had a date with this lad and he had to walk really slowly because I could only move my legs about three inches at a time. Fashions were daft then, because the week after I would be wearing about four sticky-out underskirts and look like the fairy on top of the Christmas tree.'

'The car was my Uncles – he and I used to stay up talking late at night, he was a long distance lorry driver and was mad about cars. He used to say to me "You've got a good office job – you stick to it" – he was having to work really hard on long distance lorry hauls. Anyway, he was selling this car for £90 – I'd saved about fify/sixty quid and of course it opened up a completely new life – freedom and that's what I had always wanted – freedom.'

A mode of dress which achieved the widest notoriety was without doubt the teddy boy style. Sometimes the jackets were velvet trimmed with drain-pipe trousers. Teddy boys rebelled against the 'short back and sides' hair cut and sported 'side-burns'. An essential accessory was a much flaunted comb. They appeared in their time to be anti-authoritarian and their emblem was pop music.

Top Left: 'Teddy Boys?' Chadderton Grammar School boys 1955. Left to right Tec Conn, Titch Latham, Tex Denny, Lew Walker, Dirk Reeves, Harry Kershaw, Willie Hilton, ?Matthews, Rog. Smith 'Ready to set the town on fire!'

Top Right: Washington Hotel, Blackpool 1955 Terry Conn and Neil Jones

hysterical today when I think of it, thirty years later. He's a grandpa now, dead normal and no longer on the margin of society, which was rebelling I suppose.'

An extremely popular and friendly meeting place was the King's cafe. It was here, where many young people experienced their first illicit De Reske cigarette – only to be imbued with dread if a neighbour walked in. It was a place for discussion – seeing everyone you knew, cautiously holding hands on a first date, and an oasis in the rain. Bottom of the King's broo was one of the locations to arrange to meet your date, along with the steps of the Town Hall, the Star Inn, the Chronicle Office clock, the foyer of the Gaumont or the Odeon cinema.

'When I think how I looked when I went out on Saturday nights. No wonder my dad used to comment, ≠ 'Is that a bloody boot lace, you've got on instead of a tie?" My hair had to be just one way and I would jump sky high when my mum tried lovingly to pat it. There was a lot of talk then about Teddy Boys propping the bar up, the truth was, it bloody well propped you up – you couldn't sit down in drain pipes, they were so tight. I'll tell you this, but no names, one of my friends, was misbehaving once with a girl, who was a right little raver and we'd all dared him to have a go. It took a lot of courage, because the promiscuous society was only just beginning and her father came outside shouting her in and this mate couldn't get his pants up and had to run right down the back showing his bare bum. I could still be

KINGS CINEMA
CAFE RENDEZVOUS

MENU

Special Afternoon Teas, 1/-

Bread and Butter (white or brown)		3d.
Buttered Toast		3d.
Dry Toast		2d.
Butter (per portion)		1d.
Toasted Muffin		3d.
„ Teacake		3d.
„ Scone		3d.
„ Crumpet		3d.
Scone and Butter		3d.
Welsh Rarebit		8d.
Heinz Baked Beans on Toast		8d.
„ Sardines on Toast		8d.
Boiled Egg		4d.
Poached Egg on Toast		7d.
Plate of Ham or Tongue		1/-
Pork Pie (per portion)		4d.
Lobster Salad		1/3
Crab Salad		1/-
Egg Mayonnaise		6d.
SANDWICHES :—Crab, Lobster, Salmon, Sardine, Ham, Tongue, Tomato, or Egg		6d.
Chocolate Biscuits		2d.
Assorted Pastries		3d.
Assorted Biscuits (per portion)		3d.

BEVERAGES, Etc.	
Tea, per pot, each person	4d.
Russian Tea	4d.
Coffee	4d.
Chocolate	3d.
Milk, hot or cold	4d.
Soda and Milk	4d.
Horlick's Malted Milk	4d.
Egg and Milk	5d.
Oxo and Biscuit	6d.
Bovril and Biscuit	4d.
Ovaltine	4d.
Minerals	5d.
Still Lemon	4d.
Ices	4d.
	2d. and 3d.

Cream Ices a Speciality

Highest Quality Chocolates & Cigarettes

PLEASE PAY AT THE DESK

Below: Advertising the opening of the Gaumont (minus clock!) Star Inn 1937. 'When Fenner rose up from under the floor onto the stage at the Gaumont with this magnificent machine, a spotlight would always go on him. He would start to play familiar tunes – but always came up playing his signature tune which was "Orpheus of the Underworld".'

Above: The foyer, Gaumont Cinema, Star Inn
Below: Jack Fenner at the Gaumont Organ

The cinema was once the means of escape from reality as well as a meeting place for young people. Glamour and luxury was what everyone craved and the Hollywood dream factory was the provider. This was never more evident than it was just after the war – previously when many people had been faced by unemployment, films, curiously, became more sumptious and magnificent – film stars became gods and goddesses to be worshipped from afar. Hairstyles were copied, make-up was flamboyant with blood red lipstick like a huge gash across the face.

'The queue at the Odeon grew sideways – not lengthways – everyone joined their friends – nobody seemed to bother. We would all file in noisily. If anyone was too disruptive a man came and threatened to throw them out, but it didn't happen often.'

George Nutter, behind the scenes, Gaumont Cinema, 1950's

The Odeon had a children's club and a song which was sung when they got inside.
"Every Saturday morning, where do we go?
Getting into mischief – oh dear no!
To the Mickey Mouse Club,
With our badges on,
Every Saturday morning at the O-de-on"

At the Roxy Cinema, Hollinwood, Ken Blair stepped into his father's shoes in 1950. Ken Blair senior had been at the Roxy when it opened in 1937, showing the film "Fire over England" with Flora Robson, Vivien Leigh and Laurence Olivier. The opening ceremony was on December 20th and was performed by Cllr. Tweedale who was Deputy Mayor at the time. All credit must go to the Roxy for surviving tremendous change in entertainment values and becoming the last cinema to survive.

Many Oldham children went to Saturday morning cinema prior to the 2nd World War. Every cinema held performances – usually cartoons or Flash Gordon with some nail-biting finish when it would flash on screen "Continued next week!" much to the disappointment of the cinemagoers. Photograph shows children waiting for the Gaumont to open its doors.

On Saturday afternoon we used to go to the 'Cas' off Middleton Road to see Flash Gordon. When we were playing out afterwards we would pretend we were the characters in the episode we had just seen. I was the youngest so I never got an important part. Our Mona was Dale Harden and I was a clayman. When they captured me they tied me to the lamp, it happened every week. Mrs Burley used to come and unfasten me, she'd said "Poor little bugger, have they left you again love?".'

Sonia Walton winning the title 'Oldham Cinema Queen' in 1957. Arnold Tweedale, Mayor. 'The girls all walked on in turns and then the winner was announced. The prize that I can remember was a skin handbag – not sure if there was a cash prize as well. The big treat was – FREE ENTRANCE into any Oldham Cinema – one could sweep straight in – past all the queues which there invariably was in those days, we were all such film fans.'

Above: In the Ice Cream Parlour there was a Juke Box. We would choose Frankie Laine. On Sundays at Jack Turtons the lads would say "a pint of sass" – then as they got more sophisticated would ask for a 'short Vimto!.'

Milk bars became a mecca for youngsters. Expresso coffee was the 'new' tipple and most milk or coffee bars had a juke box. When 'Rock around the Clock' was released in Britain, twelve towns banned the film. In Oldham, the Council's 'Watch Committee' met in private for over an hour before deciding not to impose a ban. The film usually provoked teenagers to leap from their seats and jive in the cinema aisle.

'I mithered and mithered to go and see 'Rock around the Clock', but my Dad didn't give in until the last minute. I think they must have heard some bad reports. Anyhow my Dad met us when it was over and we kept on jiving all the way through the market stalls which were deserted. I laugh now when I think of him saying "I'll give you some Fenning's Cooling Powders when you get in!" When you think of what films they see today, my father would turn in his grave.'

Law Swallows, which was at the bottom of George Street had listening booths which enabled you to play your requested record before deciding to buy it. The booths were soundproofed so nobody else could hear the choice of record.

'Me and Sheila bought this record – it was 4/6 – "Wrong, would it be wrong to stay, here in your arms this way". It was sung by the Continentals – we had bought it specially for this party. We used to gasp, we thought it so sexy!'

'We used to go back to Derek Baxters to listen to American Forces Network. It was on for an hour. It came from Germany and was called "Midnight in Munich". The signature tune was "Skyliner" by Charlie Barnett.'

Cigarettes were actually considered fashionable and essential to image. If you went to see a play and cigarettes were featured in it – on the back of the programme, they would be acknowledged, e.g. 'Cigarettes by Abdullah'. Even in a film, if the hero was shot or dying, someone would light a cigarette for him – rather like the last rites.

'On Sunday nights at 5 to 11 pm my Mum and Dad had gone to bed and I would switch Radio Luxembourg on – it was the top 20 – it went off at midnight. I knew my Dad kept his Woodbines in the second drawer of the sideboard – so I used to pinch one and prop the mirror up and watch myself smoking and blowing smoke rings.'

Above: Cliff Richard with the Barry Sisters at the Empire Theatre

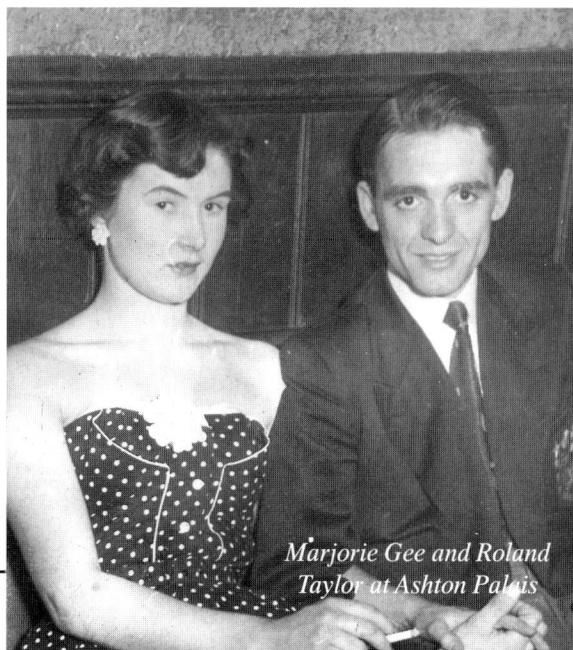

Marjorie Gee and Roland Taylor at Ashton Palais

*Beatles at the Astoria
1963*

'I remember coming home from school and my sister was lying prostrate on the settee and I said "What's the matter with you?" To which she replied "I haven't to tell anyone, but I haven't to let any boys pull me about!" A bit later, she lifted her head up rather gingerly and said, "Will it be alright if I have an orange?" It was all very mysterious and of course she had only started her periods.'

'It was a subject that was avoided. When anybody had babies, my mother used to call it 'having connections'. She would say "she's had connections". I remember her saying once, about somebody's husband "do you know the baby was only a few days old and he wanted connections!".'

'I went home and said to my Mother "Mavis Mellor's started her periods". She said "Well, she can't ride a bike, and she can't wash her hair!" You didn't ever ask "Why not?" It was thought that the blood would rush to your head and that would be terrible. You didn't have baths during a period as my Mother said "You can't wash above the knee!"'

'If your period was late, my mother would be at Shanleys on Chadderton Road for penny royal "get this down you".'

'I was just beginning to develop and this lady said "Annie,I think it's about time you had a bra" and I went home and told my mother and she brought one out that had been my Grandmas! It was a pink satin cotton thing and she was a big woman! . . . well I had to put darts and tucks everywhere, to make this great big bra fit me!.'

'I came downstairs one morning and said that I felt ill, I had stomach ache and headache and my mother was wiping the fireplace down. She never looked up or turned round from what she was doing and then she said, "Well you know what'll happen to you, don't you?" I didn't really, but when I did start my periods a few weeks later and I told her, she just said, "there's some sanitary towels in the oven" . . and that was my sex education.'

'When a shop was closing down near us, my Mother bought all their sanitary towels. They were piled high in the cupboard, I've no idea

Three subjects never discussed in the home, at least before the sixties, were, periods, having babies, and the opposite sex. Love was taken for granted and so was death – up to a point – taking the age of the departed in account.

The facts of life were learned usually from an enlightened friend and listened to with disbelief, always relating the information to one's Mother and Father and the King and Queen. The friend was remembered forever – even recognised for this amazing knowledge, many years later in the supermarket, when the informant herself would have forgotten all about it.

how many packets there must have been. Anyhow any hopes she had never materialised, because I became pregnant. I was 19 and terrified, I went to the doctors' on my own, but a neighbour saw me and told her. It was all hell let loose. I had to get married immediately – in fact she didn't speak to me until after I was married. It was doomed from the start, I hadn't led a promiscuous life, becoming pregnant seemed like a punishment. We had to go and live with two old men, we had nothing. In fact my Dad bought my ring . . . and my husband . . . well – he was all black leather and chains, and knives over the bed – even a noose. It was a nightmare and when I'd had the baby, I packed my bag one night and moved in with my married sister!'

People became very conscious of the threat of nuclear war in the fifties. In 1952 after the Americans exploded their first hydrogen bomb on the Marshall Islands followed by a more powerful version at Bikini Atoll in 1954, the Russions retaliated with their own H-Bomb. It was inevitable that Britain would follow suit and they did in 1957. There was growing opposition from the Labour Government and from many other directions and this resulted in the birth of the nuclear disarmament movement. The first large protest took place at Easter in 1958, when hundreds of people walked to Aldermaston, supported by many Church leaders.

The Festival of Britain in 1951 acted as a showcase for most British designs. It was a stimulus to the Arts; and painters and sculptors were invited to provide works for exhibition. Among them were the sculptors, Henry Moore, Barbara Hepworth and Jacob Epstein and artists John Piper, Ben Nicholson, Graham Sutherland and Lucien Freud. The festival was responsible for bringing new life into a grey world, and gave a defiant shrug of the shoulders to the past years of austerity. In many ways it symbolised a futuristic Britain. The Skylon was the most distinctive feature, pointing a sculptural finger up into the sky. There was the Bailey Bridge built by the War Office, and a pavilion devoted to the nation's new toy, which was television.

Open plan schemes appeared, which fitted in with the idea of an informality of life-style. Doors were flushed and interior walls knocked down to give the look of spaciousness. The word 'Contemporary' described almost everything desirable.

Decorative laminate was used enthusiastically, and textured wall surfaces, furniture with splayed black legs and brass feet, were all characteristics of fifties interiors. It became popular to define different areas of the house by using different wallpapers – sometimes as many as four in one room. Abstract designs for furnishing fabrics were often bizarre and occasionally there would be an uncompromising brashness which typified the decade.

1953 celebrated the first Coronation in history to be televised. People in Oldham had T.V. parties if they were fortunate enough to know someone who had a television.

'We all sat round the sideboard, on which the tele' reigned as supreme as the Queen. We had our backs to the fire, there would be about sixteen of us all squinting at the 9" black and white, it wasn't sharp. Nobody thought of moving the damn sideboard. You didn't do things like that, even for the Coronation.'

On the same day people heard that Edmund Hilary had conquered Everest, which reassured people that this was a decade when anything was possible.

A great deal of the fashion produced in the 60's was narcissistic. The mini which appeared so daringly in 1967 was looked upon with disdain, many women vowing it would never catch on. Although its time in the sun was as brief as its style, for the young it was like a breath of fresh air and had about as much substance. For the first time ever, the young were about to lead the old.

C.N.D. parading in Oldham on a Saturday afternoon in November 1962 before attending a rally on the West Street site.

Dancing Years

The first place I went dancing was to Leesfield School. I was 16. My father was very strict and I had to walk all up Lane Head, and I had to be by the pub – the Old Clock, before they turned out, otherwise I would be in trouble, so I used to run over the fields at the back, so he wouldn't see me. It was easily a mile with no lights and very lonely, but it was familiar to me so I was never frightened. If my friend and me met two boys I would tell them I lived in Lees – where my friend lived and then I used to have to run like hell home.

We then started to go to all the other dance halls – Hill Stores mostly – but also to Froggatts, the Embassy, King Street Stores, Lees Store, the Y.M.C.A. – (that was where you go down to B&Q now) it was only a small place but nice and friendly, and one on Elliot Street – nearly always ended up with a fight – we would be stood on forms cheering them on .. and the Oldham Palais on Copsterhill Rd – (now the Salvation Army). The Savoy, and Waterhead Mechanics, and Mossley Mechanics – we really got around. I didn't used to tell them at home where we were going – I daren't have told my father. I was only eighteen when my father died and by then we moved down to Lees. I found I could tell my Mother the truth then. When my father was living I told some awful lies – I had to be in before 11 pm – well the dances didn't finish till 12 – so I would say I missed the bus. The Oldham Rugby dances at Hill Stores were the best and they were 2/6 and I didn't have much money, but I went out with a boy who had two complimentary tickets – just the one night – I didn't go out with him again and that night I was late and got into trouble.'

Garforth Street Novelty Orchestra in the 1920s, Jack Nelson is 2nd from the left

'I was always interested in music. There was a trunk in my bedroom and I found some sheet music in it, so I taught myself in an amateurish way.'

'My brother played with Ken Gibson's Accordian swingsters in Sunday school hops. I used to listen, I loved it. Through my brother I started to play for dances at the Conservative Club on Union Street I think they were one short and so I went home for my sax' and I got 10 shillings at the end of the night – that started me off I suppose.

I started to play with Rodney Benson's 'Academy Swing Ten', and played for six months. It was the Sunday school scene, which was really a stopping off scene. The young ladies were always nicely dressed – observations made you aware of the social strata. When we played at the Savoy – we would meet there for rehearsing at 10 am and after I would go with them into the Regent, drinking draft bass out of champagne glasses. Thinking about it, my parents were quite remarkable – very bohemian in that respect – very liberal. I would play until 11 pm in the evening and I was only a kid'.

'My mother came into contact with Tommy Green, I don't know how, but he was a sergeant in the specials during the war and a professional musician off Variety stage. He listened to me and I joined the Civil Defence Orchestra.'
'I also played in Ashton for Cyril Blake – the lads weren't allowed in without a tie. Alan Roper played then – I think he was probably one of the best arrangers in this country for TV themes and programmes – it all rubbed off on me. Ronnie Hazelhurst played the trumpet. There was one chap who played – he lived on Park Rd – Harry Bowden Smith, played mostly in Royton and Shaw. He started running trips abroad – he was quite ambitious – he eventually became 'Arrowsmith. When we were playing at the Union Club, it was another world. We played for the Freemasons' dances etc., I have such a lot of lovely memories of playing.'

'Auld Lang Syne' – Midnight, Hill Stores, New Years Eve. One of the few times in the year when an extension was granted.

'Hill Stores – it always had the edge on other places. We used to line up for tickets – they had some big bands come along sometimes. Even during the war – I remember going to see Eric Winstone at Hill Stores. The R.A.F. band came as well – there would be about three or four hundred in that hall every week and for Christmas Eve and New Year's Eve – you used to have to line up for your tickets to make sure you got in. Before the dance halls we used to go to Sunday School Socials – as they called them – they were dances of course – but you sort of graduated to the dance halls in Oldham as you grew up, ninety per cent of my mates, met their wives at Hill Stores.'

'When I met Dorothy at Hill Stores, she lived at Rhodes Hill, (Lees) so it was quite a walk for me from Hill Stores to Lees and back home, so I would be coming up Edge Lane Road about 1.30am on Sunday morning and I had to be up again at 8a.m to serve on the altar at Church! But walking was safe, whatever time it was. One thing that was always drummed into us – when we met girls – was to find out if they were Roman Catholics – as I've got older – to me it doesn't make any difference – you had to find out which Church they went to, they might say "I go to Saint Annes or Saint Patricks" – or somewhere, and then you used to drop 'em – it was ridiculous.'

Top: Christmas Eve, Hill Stores 1954

Above: Stained glass window in the dance hall at Hill Stores

'I remember Jack being called up in the army – he had advertised for a tenor sax', it was about 1940. I auditioned at Hill Stores on a Sunday morning. When I was playing and got a 10 shilling note I felt rich. My wage for all week was only 11 shillings and sometimes I would play three nights a week – I'd earn 30 shillings in all – it was wonderful. Lads would meet in the local pub – I was, at that time, the tender age of 15.'

'From the stage we could see the scene change of course. During the war the uniforms appeared, at this time occasionally the sirens went. Early on in the war – we did clear the floor – but the young people hadn't got much in their lives then and the band leader used to give them the choice, "Shall we carry on?" and they would all shout "Yes!".'

'Jack tried to keep us all on the straight and narrow – he didn't drink and never swore – he was a marvellous example. He would say to the lads when they were eyeing some girl up, "you're married" – keep your eyes off 'em and concentrate on your music!" I played with Jack Nelson for about 10 years.'

'It was wonderful to sit up there on the stage at Hill Stores and see all the well-dressed girls. They really did look gorgeous with all their lovely dresses. I don't think that anywhere, I have seen prettier, and smarter girls that there was in Oldham at that time, their hair shone and they looked so clean and scrubbed in the 50's'.

'A lot of the musicians did dance and they would have been looking enviously at the girls on the dance floor while they were playing. It would be a stroke of luck if the band leader could get the pianist to play and the drummer to play and one instrumentalist for a waltz and there was a chance for the musician to go on the dance floor and pick up the girl he had been weighing up all night and perhaps ask to take her home.'

'Froggatts, about 1937 – you had to have a long dress on – it probably stopped during war time – but Hill Stores on New Year's Eve was very special. A little old man used to go across the floor when the old year faded and a fairy used to come in at the other side – it was wonderful – the band playing "the bells are ringing the Old Year out and the New Year in". I went to the Savoy before Tommy Smith took it over, even before Jack Nelson was there – I can't remember the name of the band, but you could have a meal there – downstairs – cooked things, sausage and that. When the war was on, my sister-in-law and me went to the Savoy one night and met two Yanks – they couldn't dance – they just shuffled but we walked down Yorkshire St. with them, all the time terrified that someone may see us – but we got on the bus at Mumps and left them. It was after that – I give over going dancing, it was too tempting – I was married. I had two friends whose husbands were away and we used to go to the pictures and afterwards we'd talk for ages at Lilian's and I would walk home – sometimes at two am in the morning and never think anything of it and there was soldiers at the Further Hey and the Glen – but you were safe then.'

'When I was a kid aged between six years to 12 years I used to accompany bands like Geraldo, Jack Jackson, Roy Fox, Maurice Winnick and Carroll Gibbons when they were on the wireless – using the old fashioned fireplace to drum on, then me and Norman Mills, who played the piano accordian started to play at clubs and little dances – we were recommended by word of mouth. We were only 14 and would earn 2/6 (12^1/2p) from 7pm - 11pm. It gave us a bit of money, and it helped to purchase better quality drums when enough money had been saved.

I started drumming when I was in the Boy's Brigade – then I joined St. John's Ambulance Pipe Band. I never had a lesson in my life. To have music lessons was considered very privileged. My mother and father couldn't afford to buy me a kit – but when I left school at 14 I used to go round the second hand shops and buy bits and pieces and I managed to put a kit together.'

'I was playing at the Y.M.C.A. at Rhodes Bank when I was 16, Harry Woodcock was looking for a drummer. One or two of the lads in Harry's band had played in Tommy Smith's Black Bandits – they formed their own unit. Tommy Smith went to Croydon Palais with his band which was on the Mecca Circuit. (like the Ritz) While I was with Harry Woodcock, Tommy Smith came to visit occasionally – called in to see his old pals and one Saturday he came in and said his drummer – a local lad – Norris Grundy had left to join Lou Preager's band at Hammersmith Palais. Tommy asked me to replace Norris, but I had to refuse – my Mum and Dad were dead against it, they thought it a precarious career and anyway I had a job at Ferranti – which paid me 10shillings a week!'

Top: Rex Kane's band, playing at Hill Stores Dec. 17th 1948. Eddie Cooke was the M.C.

Right: 'Blue Metros' Hill Stores 1954

'Hill Stores – well, it was lovely, dancing to Jack Nelson and his Blue Metros. The stage had footlights and we used to pile our handbags in one corner and when the dance was over girls would shout "just pass me that one" . . . etc. I can't remember any being stolen – nobody ever thought about the possibility. If you had your eye on someone, you sweated until he came over before someone beat him to it. Occasionally there was an 'excuse me', when a boy would tap another on the shoulder if he was dancing with the girl he wanted and she would change partners. A popular girl could be excused at least 20 times in one dance.'

'At Hill Stores we never paid for the cloakroom – we simply left everything and coat hooks were piled with everybody's belongings. We weren't afraid to leave our things and I don't remember anything going missing.'

'Blue Metros' Hill Stores 1958. Front Row (L-R) Jack Clavingom, Ray Osbaldeston, Jack Nelson, Arthur Beckett, Jean Taylor, Walter Jennings. Back Row (L-R) Len Higham, Johnny Hodinott, Jack Bell, Jack Mitchell, Harvey Crossland, Harry Ogden.

Left: Blue Metros

Below:
White Star Band, Froggatts.
Frank Thompson, Tommy Green,
Freddie Hart and others

'Going home from Hill Stores was almost as much fun as the dancing bit. We would all pile out into the warm petrol-scented night, laughing at – we didn't know what – just because we were untroubled I guess – before marriage and mortgage. We saw many a drunk being linked home by the bobby, the odd couple having a quick fumble in the doorway, but mostly singing and enjoying the untrammelled freeness of youth.'

During the waltzes a large crystal ball, high up in the centre of the room, would slowly turn round and the impression was of snow flakes circling the room – it was quite romantic. It was always over at 11.45 p.m. Saturday night, because dancing on Sunday wasn't allowed. At Christmas and New Year, dance halls would apply for an extension until 1 a.m. Nobody walked home alone, it was noisy but great fun.

The Savoy with Tommy Smith "I'd like to get you on a slow boat to China", and "I would gather stars out of the blue, for you, for you," was open Monday evenings as well as Saturday and Sunday.

Froggatts at Bottom of the Moor was also popular and young people would change – sometimes Hill Stores, sometimes Froggatts, which was also open on Wednesday evenings. The young people who went to Froggatts were fractionally older, but 25 was considered old in the 50's if you weren't courting.

'There was certainly a kind of social class hierarchy among the adherents of the dance halls. Some were classed as low class dives. Froggatts had a good social class mix as far as I remember. I danced with milkmen, trainee accountants, tool fitters, teachers etc. and we girls had a similar spread – office workers, shop assistants, nurses, students and so on. Froggatts being the place for the older end was sometimes described as the bachelors/spinsters last hope!'

'There was a man on the door at Froggatts and if you were dressed in something that looked like a two-piece, he would examine it, to see if it was two pieces. I had this really nice costume once, I can see it now, but I spent the night before the dance stitching it together and he couldn't tell, so I got in.'

Above Left: White Star band, Drummer, Cliff Jackson, Centre Frank Thomson and Piano, Ike Stansfield.

Above Right: Jacky Allan singing at the Savoy in the 1950's.

Below: "Beginners Steps"

'My dad used to practice in the house when he was in the White Star band. He played Sax and Clarinet and he would play records and accompany them. I remember most "Artie Shaw's clarinet concerto" and he played that over and over again; and I have the record, but can't play it now, it is so upsetting. Unfortunately my dad left us when I was eleven and of course I didn't understand – you don't at that age – but he was my dad and I loved him, so naturally I was upset and we always kept in touch.'

'I remember wanting to go to the Savoy which was right in the centre of the town and consequently in the centre of all the activity. I'm talking about the early 50's when Oldham was always very busy and lit up for all hours. I had to pluck up courage to ask my Dad if I could go to the Savoy – I was nineteen years old. There was something about the Savoy, it was a bit intimate – a bit like a night club. In fact, I think you had to be a member at one time.
'When Tommy Smith played 'When the saints come marching in', it always brought the house down.'

'Before the war, Jack Nelson's band played at the Savoy and Fred Pickles, who owned the building promised Jack that he could have the first offer of the Savoy if they sold – but after the war Tommy Smith came back to Oldham and bought it. Jack Nelson was very let down, but it worked out OK, because the kids at Hill Stores really loved him.'

'I was always crazy about dancing. My friend and I used to go and watch them dance at Ashton Palais and I would long for someone to ask me, but I was only fourteen and at that time, a fourteen year old looked like a fourteen year old. But it was then that I decided I wanted to dance.
I met Albert Billington on holiday in the Isle of Man, it would be Oldham Wakes and I ended up becoming his dancing partner and wife.'
'We came to Ascroft St. in 1934 and we had no money at all. It was owned at that time by the Turner family. A dancing instructor in Manchester set us up in business and we worked very hard. It was an awful time to

BEGINNERS' STEPS

by
Mr. & Mrs. A. Billington
Ascroft Street · Oldham

...KSTEP.

...o rise, but second step is taken on ball of foot.
...y. There is no sway.
28

QUICKSTEP.

LADY'S STEPS.

Zig-Zag.

Commence and finish with back to L.O.D.

R.F. back, turning body to Left .... S.
Close L.F. to R.F., turning on Right heel ..... S.
R.F. forward O.P. Take this step across the body .... S.
L.F. to side across the L.O.D. ...... S.
Brush R.F. to L.F. then step back on R.F. S.
C.B.M. on 1 and 5, slight on 5.
...o rise, but the fourth step is taken on ball of foot.
Sway. There is no sway.

29

Above: What a tale it could tell!' Billington's Dance Academy, with the familiar seats lining the walls.

start, because of the depression and we had to ask for time as we hadn't earned enough money to pay the rates. Things had started to improve, then the war came with all its problems – blackout, air-raids and parents not allowing girls to come out during the blackout.'

After the war, Oldham's youngsters were mad about dancing and it was a wonderful meeting place for boys and girls – many met the person they married while they were at Billingtons. I suppose we were a bit old-fashioned because the girls couldn't have pass-outs and the boys could, but we looked on it as a protection really. It was rather like home from home – we knew everyone who came and when we saw weddings in the Weekly Chronicle, we took great pride in being someway responsible.'

'You would be looking forward to Saturday all week. At Hill Stores you always had to have a ticket, because it got quite crowded, but at Billington's you went early if you wanted to go upstairs. You walked through the cafe to the cloakroom and some girls would have their curlers in. They'd start getting ready, there and then. They had this enormous settee in the cafe part. It wasn't licensed of course. A lot of the boys used to go out to the pub in the interval and the girls would dance together or sit and gossip, it was considered a bit common for girls to go in the pubs.'

'We were friendly with a lot of young people from Saddleworth and one girl in particular lived in Diggle and she had to get the last train from Oldham. It meant coming out of Billington's before the dance was over and running down Clegg St., because the train left at 11.10pm and arrived in Delph, I think about 20 to 12 midnight. The guard used to shout "Are they all here?" We would tell him they were and when the train set off, one or two lads would come flying down the platform and we would drag them into the compartment with their ties – it was amazing that nobody was ever hurt and nothing was ever made of it.'

Dance at Chadderton Town Hall, 1950's

'I think I probably went to the Majestic because it was near home. On Tuesday nights it was 1/–d. A man we called Pop Lloyd ran the dances, he was very well known and lived near the Spotted Cow on Bent.
At weekends, they would come in coaches, they would all pile in and in the interval it would be the Lancashire Vaults on Manchester St. or the King Bill on York St. We had a chip shop and the coach driver used to come to the supper bar out of the way. They would come back in real fighting mood – they weren't really used to drinking those lads.'

'A coach went to Blackpool some Saturdays. It would leave at 4 pm and we would go to the Winter Gardens and dance to Ted Heath. The singers were Dicky Valentine, Lita Rosa and Dennis Lotis. There was always something special about a big dance band, and this great globe in the middle turning round and flashing lights . . . like, everywhere you went then, there was a dance-hall – holidays or anywhere – you just stuck your hand-bag on the stage, you could leave anything, it would still be there when you went for it. In Oldham – we followed Jack Nelson – if he wasn't playing at Hill Stores and going to Chaddy Town Hall – we'd follow him.'

Below: Ready for the dance' Saturday night c. 1962

Above Left: Johnny Peters and the Crestas, Butlins Holiday Camp. Rock 'n' Calypso Ballroom 1962.

This postcard was sent home, and the message on the back reads "Having a lovely time. The weather is great. That cross in the corner of the ballroom, well that's our corner where we meet after every dance. I'm sunburned. Lots of Love, Joyce"

'When Reginald Dixon started to play "I do like to be beside the seaside", the atmosphere was so friendly, it was almost indescribable. Within seconds, the floor was crowded and was like that every night. It was such a massive place, you had to always arrange to meet your friends at a certain pillar or you may not have seen them again all night.'

Left: Jack Nelson's band playing at an open air concert at Strinesdale Hospital 1954

I DO LIKE TO BE BESIDE THE SEASIDE

Going Away

Fifty years ago when the people of Oldham went on holiday, it was hardly ever to pastures new. The destination was usually familiar, with the landlady known to all the family. It may have been slightly warmer and dryer without the looming Pennines, but the clothing worn would not differ much from that worn at home.

Once a year, cases were taken down from the top of the wardrobe, some of them exhaling a strong odour of camphor. Fine weather was the item most longed for, it was wonderful to say on returning home, "We never wore our coats once!" To fill the lungs with sea-air was a cure for all winter ills. The coveted sixpence at the first sign of Blackpool Tower was desired by most children and curiously, almost minutes after stepping off the train, a card would be sent home saying, "Arrived safely, wish you were here".

Above: Oldham Wakes 1937, Mumps Station
*Left: 'Paddling in waders and **always** wearing hats!' Blackpool c. 1926. Hotel Metropole in background.*
Below left: Peggy Laister and Harry Andrew building a sandcastle by North Pier, Blackpool c. 1927.
Below right: Dennis and Moreen Wood with their mother on holiday in Cleveleys, 1937.

Left: Doing your own at Blackpool,
'We always stayed at South Shore. We did our own, had a cupboard allotted to us in the sideboard in the dining room. We bought in when we arrived and gave the food for our dinner to the landlady each day, and she would cook it for us. Sago pudding and rice pudding was brought in for afters, some boarding houses did no afters. Also, we always had nice scented soap for that week, but no hot water, just a large jug and bowl on the wash stand.'

OPPOSITE PAGE:
Background photo: Bathing Pool, Blackpool 1920s
Top left: Holidays, 1920s. Eva Smith on right.
'If you stayed at home, there was always the Wakes and little treats, like new sandals, or staying up late.'
Top right: On the Wakes, Eva Lomas with Frank and Lucy Sudds and A.N. Other 1923.
Below top: Near Gynn Square, Blackpool c 1925. Nora Halliwell wearing waders.
'Every year we went to my Grandfather's,' He had retired to Blackpool, originally he was a butcher on Yorkshire St. and when he became a widower, he was looked after by the youngest of the family, as was the usual arrangement in those days.'

Above: The Isle of Man c1930. Oldham people on holiday. Ann Smith with friends.

Left: Bridlington. Heading for the sands.

Below centre: Betty Millett, New Brighton, Oldham Wakes 1930s
'Before we went on holiday, my mother would be up all night, washing and getting our clothes ready. She just never went to bed that night – we didn't question it at all, because she had always done it. We hadn't got any special holiday clothes, so she would wash and iron everything we had worn. Considering we had no central heating or dryer, it must have been a mammoth task, but we always managed to get off on time. A wonderful poster on the station advertised **"New Brighton – Where ocean liners pass your bedroom window"** *– not past ours they didn't'.*

Above: 'Making for the sands' Florry Wood and Marjorie 1930's. 'On the sands' – Marjorie.
Left: 'Helping Mum over the rocks' c1928.

Right: Oldham Wakes.
1930s
Muriel Chantler, Mildred
Schofield, Joan Coleman
and Edith Hall.

Below: Waiting for the ferry
to Ilfracombe from
Minehead 1930, Oldham
Wakes.

'I went on holiday with a great aunt – my Grandma's sister and Mr. Henthorn's taxi would take us to the station. We never went on the sands, as Aunty Harriet had what was known as a "white leg". I never saw it, because although I shared her room, I always had to turn my face to the wall when she was getting undressed. I didn't mind not going on the sands, because I would read, Sunny Stories, . . . anything.'

Bevy of beauties –
Oldham Wakes.
New Brighton 1930s

'At the boarding house, there was always a notice up in the hall. It said "Leave your buckets and spades in the vestibule". When we went to buy a bucket and spade we would take ages choosing. My Mum would have said "You only have 1/6", and the price would determine the size. They were tin – the buckets and spades and the designs and colours on the buckets were lovely. If we had any money over we'd buy a bundle of flags.'

Above top: 'Walkie Snap', outside Central Station, Blackpool. Alan Wolstencroft with his mum. Left: Near the rocks at Bispham – Sheila, Margaret and Gavin Struthers c 1936.

Below left and right: 'If we were going from Werneth Station, my Dad had to carry the bags and cases all over Featherstall Road, He would keep changing arms and stopping to have a rest. Parents went to enormous lengths then so their children could have a holiday. If the bucket and spade hadn't rusted much from the year before, you were allowed to take it on holiday with you and of course, the railway stations were crowded and you'd be weaving in and out of the people and cutting your Mum's legs with the spade. It is a wonder nobody got blood poisoning because there was always some rust.'

'Spot the Green Final'
Oldham holiday group
outside boarding house.

Below: Peggy Lo... s...
on a car in a ...
moment at Bla...

'One night, it was always the highlight of the week, we went to the Spa ballroom and I would dance with my Dad or anyone we had made friends with. I had a pink satin dress that went with me every year and Miss Wellbourne used to iron it for the special night. It must have gone shorter and shorter as the years went on. I wore it with sandals and socks. We always made lots of friends on holiday, because when people got back from the sands, they congregated in the front garden of the boarding house. I would go off and play somewhere nearby, you were quite safe, everyone was so trusting then.'

Below: Eileen Keane and Jean Hallett, Prestatyn Holiday Camp, 1940s. 'Our Eileen and Jean had their pins in nearly all the time to curl their hair and one day they came into the dining hall in turbans so they wouldn't have to take them out and my Dad went mad and made them go and comb their hair. I probably sat there looking smug because my hair was naturally curly.'

Above left: Fred Dixon dancing with his mum on Central Pier, Blackpool, 1949.
Above right: Just after the war, although people had cameras, films were still
very scarce and the only photographs were 'walkie snaps' – everyone would
take turns walking towards the camera – occasionally changing clothes and
queueing again for a second photo.

Above: Testing the water at Bournemouth.

Right: Hotel in Newquay with 1950's
decor, Doreen and Peter Smith.

Above: Olga Cunliffe and Beryl Goodwin – Isle of Man
'We were both 18 and worked together at the Belgrave Mill. I met this lad called Norman, he had a centre parting and I thought he was so sophisticated. He came from far afield and that gave him an allure – when I think now – it was only Sheffield, it seemed miles away to us, we were so unworldly and had never travelled away from home, except when we went on holiday.'

'I went to Lido de Jesolo in Italy. Most young people at that time were going to Butlins or Squires Gate or even the Isle of Man, so it was a very adventurous thing for two innocent girls. We met the two girls on the left of the photograph during our holiday and sort of 'pal'd' together. We didn't have any alcoholic drinks and were very wary of the Italian men – we had heard so many tales. Our money ran out in the first few days and the older people on the tour were always treating us, buying us a coke and a cream cake. The young man on the left is an Italian.'

Below: Typical Oldham Wakes weather, Cornwall 1965.

Oldham Wakes, Saturday morning before boarding the coach 1953.

North Western bus stop outside the Museum on Greaves Street, Oldham Wakes 1967.

Butlins

In its heyday as many as 11,500 holiday makers would visit Butlins, Filey. Its area spread over 250 acres and provided every possible activity desired for a holiday without a dull moment . . . or a quiet one. The camp was situated within easy reach of the beach, but far away from the town or any other distraction.

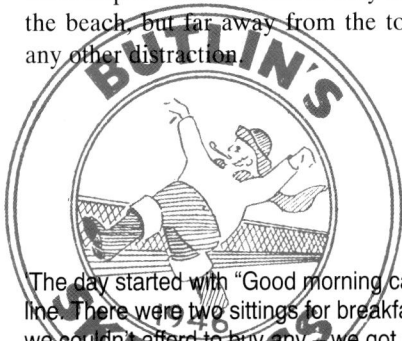

The day started with "Good morning campers" coming over the tannoy, down every chalet line. There were two sittings for breakfast, so if you didn'tget up – you missed it. Because we couldn't afford to buy any – we got up – we went to the 'morning coffee dance' – the 'afternoon tea dance' and of course we danced every evening, until 'goodnight campers'. In between we joined in every activity and at the end of the week, came home more tired than when we went! The camp at Filey was reputed to have the longest bar in the world – 198ft. It sported 30 barmaids and 24 waitresses!'

Billy Butlin must have been extremely enterprising, perhaps he was a man with a vision . . . whatever it was, it certainly paid off. After the war, he eventually bought up all the deserted army and navy base camps and by dividing up the dormitories with breeze block, he created chalets for holiday makers, and made himself one of the first post-war millionaires.

'Pwhelli was H.M.S. Glendower and Skegness, H.M.S. Royal Arthur. Clacton was another Naval camp and Filey, another base. For specific reasons during war - time, these camps were all situated near the coast, consequently, ideal venues for holiday camps.'

Above: Audrey Nutter 'Redcoat' Butlin's Skegness, 1951.
Left: Butlins, Filey – Geoff Bradbury and Albert Shore, 1949.

'To think, four of us lived in this small room for a week. We went for a few years!'

Main picture: Barry Island. Vivien Lees with her Dad, Harry. 1960.
Above top:Brenda Booth and Pat Parry – 1952.
Above: Werneth Station 1955 going to Butlins. Barbara Froman, Barbara Hilton, Irene Thompson, Pat Mann, Jean Taylor & others.

Right: This plane which was built in 1929, was stripped and boxed up during the war. After the war it was rebuilt and did 10/– trips (50p) at Butlins, Filey. The same aeroplane was featured in a book about the worst aircraft in history.

'At Pwhelli – Butlins, I met a lad called Alan Brown who came from Macclesfield. He was with a friend and we were so impressed, because they had these two powerful motor-bikes and took us a ride on them. We had no crash helmets and neither had they! Warning bells rang when he put his hand on my bust and I avoided him after that, we were so young and naive then.'

Below: Butlins, Pwhelli, Oldham Wakes 1962. Lesley and Joan (bottom left hand corner) watching day-time activities, but preparing for the evening's dance.

Above: 'In the dining room at Butlins, there had to always be eight persons on a table, so if less than eight went as a family or friends you had to join somebody else. It was always very noisy, but cheerful – if somebody dropped a plate everybody clapped and when a contest was won, the winners had to stand on their chairs until the score was counted and a lot of cheering went on.'

'I volunteered for the Navy when I was 16$\frac{1}{2}$ years old and the curious thing is – if it hadn't been raining that day – it might never have happened. If you worked outside, you were rained off when the weather was bad and this certain Tuesday, two of my mates Chris Wright and Kenny Scott, had Tuesday afternoon off as their half day. At weekend they had decided to join up. The war was over anyway, so we didn't feel any threat. Whether their influence was strong I don't know, they were a bit older than me . . . however, we went to Dover Street in Manchester and me and Kenny joined the Navy and Chris joined the R.A.F. When I got home, my mother played hell, she tried all ways to stop me, but I was determined.
    The procedure was, I was instructed to meet this Petty Officer on the station at Manchester, who gave me a railway ticket and packet of sandwiches and it was to take me to Filey Camp in Yorkshire – little did I know that a few years ahead I would meet my wife at the same camp when it was bought by Billy Butlin. It was bitter cold – November. I slept in my overcoat and there was still barbed wire on the beaches.'

Let's have a day out

Top: Oldham cycling lads – in Cheshire.
Above: Springhead Conservative Club day trip, 1920s.
Right: Day trip to Blackpool in 1926. Amy Kent in the middle of her Aunty and Uncle on the front seat. 'I remember my Aunty Amy having the most lovely clothes, she was very fashionable and I enjoyed being with them both.'
Below: Hollinwood Cosmopolitan Society cars at Partington on a day trip in 1926 for poor children. Hollinwood Councillors were members, all the cars were locally owned.

1st Club Tour YMCA, 1926

Cycling trip from the Oldham Y.M.C.A. 1926.

"After a good day's cycling"– one lad was a butcher and couldn't join us, until he had finished, but he used to bring us some food and we had a right good tuck in.'

Above: Trip to Southport from the Welfare on Ripponden Road.,1928.
'It was funny to see what we took with us – we were only going for a day, and it took us half a day to get there. Notice – there are no fellas on the trip like there would be today, that is one thing that has improved, fathers are more involved with their children these days. Imagine, no disposable nappies and no plastic bags – what a toil!'

Above: Tom Gillespie and two friends. They walked to Blackpool and back and had a bit left over to have their photograph taken. It was the first time Tom had ever seen the sea. He was 15 years old and determined he was going to see it.

Left: Lees family and Hewlett family on a day out.

'My mother and father's bike had no sidecar. They bought it in 1926. It was 2¼ H.P. and had an Oldham registration. My Aunty and Uncle's bike was more powerful, 500 H.P. but had a side car. I used to go with them, only on my push-bike and I always kept up.'

105

Above: 'Front House' Springhead. Day trip 1930s, the landlady is wearing a pinny. The May Queen is Marian Rose.

Left: Oldham group of the North West 'side-car' club, on a day out.

Below Left: Grotton Lido 1936.
'We would pack some butties and go to Grotton for the day, we had a wonderful time but it was often cold. There are houses there now, I wonder what happened to it.'

Below Middle: Hopkin Mill, Lees. Margaret and Frank Treadwell with the Battersbys. 'We used to take a picnic for the day and catch sticklebacks.'

Below Right: Ladies trip to New Brighton from the Whitestone Inn, 1936.

NEW OLDHAMERS

'He ain't heavy – he's my brother'

Once upon a time we were all incomers – or our parents were – or our grandparents. Many arrived here with only the richness of memory and wisdom. They came for a variety of reasons. Some came because they wanted to walk free, some because they were invited, others because they had no choice, many because they wanted to stay British, all with one common aim – to work.

Both refugees and immigrants, as they eagerly tried to come to terms with English society, experienced some kind of racism or the trauma of refugee status.

'I arrived in Oldham in the middle of 1954 after finishing my studies at Salford Tech. which is now Salford University. Before going back to Pakistan which was what I intended to do, I want some experience and the best place I thought was the cotton mill, but they would not recognise my special diploma. All they wanted was a labouring force – so I was taken on as a labourer at the Trent Mill in Shaw.

The manager said I was wasting my time, labouring and although I had technical knowledge, I need practical knowledge and I continued my studies in stripping and grinding. At that time I was I think, the only Pakistani in Oldham. I felt very lonely – nobody to talk to – but I had one advantage – I could speak English, people wouldn't believe this however, I know because they would speak so loud and I had to convince them many times that I could read and write, I didn't argue I just got on with it.

I eventually became a training officer and at that time I was living at 77 Queens Road as a lodger. One day when I came home from work, the man had let the room to someone else and all my baggage was outside. I managed to find another room but my previous landlord's wife told me two weeks later, she said. "Yes, there was a letter for you from abroad and my husband has sent it back – *addressee not known".* I tried to say that they knew I was only in the same road. That letter was offering me a job, to come back to Pakistan and I lost that opportunity for ever.'

Kahil Mir

'Not chance of birth or place has made us friends,
Being often times of different tongues and nations,
But the endeavour for the self same ends.
With the same hopes and fears and aspirations.'

Longfellow

Farouk Mir – Alexandra Park 1967 wearing her wedding shawl.

'I came to Oldham in 1967 to my husband, who I had married in Pakistan, our mothers were sisters. The first thing I noticed was in the evenings, it was so cold. When you are in Pakistan you read about England and mostly it is London, and I never knew that England would be like Oldham was. It seems England to me now of course, but then all those black buildings, it was quite a shock!'

'Most of the people in Oldham come from small Pakistan villages where the wife was working – in the fields perhaps, but when they had brought them here and provided what they were short of, they would rather them not be working and they perhaps wanted to have a lot of protection for them because they were in a strange country – there must be some explanation.'

'When my husband came home from work one day I say to him "I want to find some kind of job, I want to learn the language", and one day he said "I've got a job for you, it is a part-time job and you will get £6 a week." I wanted to know what the job was and he told me, it was to go to the park twice a day, he was going to pay me to walk round the park. If you are married – your husband – he feels then that he should be the provider.'

'It was difficult and not being able to speak the language, I felt very lonely and when my husband had gone out to work I thought to myself "how is this day going to finish?" It was a long day to get through on my own. My English actually started when I took my son to school and I met an English lady with her little boy.'

'I knew how difficult it had been for me so I started to collect a few ladies together and talk to them after speaking to the local Vicar. By then I had some confidence – I had learned some English. I formed a group, there was one West Indian, one Italian, one Pakistani and myself. It started in my living room.'

Below: Alexandra School – Azhar Mir and Garth Whittle centre front who became firm friends.

AZHAR. K. MIR 2 YRS
HAPPY BIRTHDAY
I DO NOT TALK

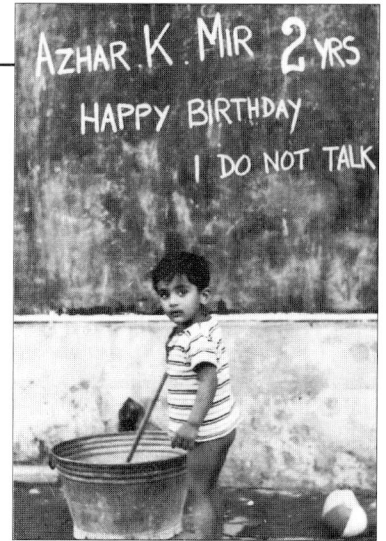

Above: Taken when Kahil took his son back to Pakistan for a visit and to see his relatives.
Left: Out for the day with the Whittles. Garth and Azhar at Delph.

'We came to Oldham in 1957 after living in London for a short time. We thought it would be easier to find work and cheaper accommodation. We had one child then who had been born in Barbados, but we left him in the care of his Grandma, until we got established. When you are young, time is an eternity and we planned to stay for five years. At that time the British Government were encouraging West Indians to come to England – there was a lot of propaganda about it. They were targetting the young people to train as nurses or transport workers. We were told what type of clothing we should bring and how much money – the minimum was £10. We also had to undergo stringent medicals. In Oldham, we lived in one room for a short time, but we wanted to send for our son, we missed him so much. We managed to save £100, it was very difficult and put down a deposit on our first house on Horsedge Street.' *(The actual house where Ellen Brierley, one of Oldham's Mayors, was brought up.)*

'Other immigrants would give you lodgings, because they understood how difficult it had been for them. You weren't expected to have any children when you were in lodgings. At our first place, when she saw I was pregnant, she said she needed the room. We were still haunted by the notices we saw in London which said 'No children, No Jews, No Irish' . . . but Oldham was more humane, and of course, once you have a house, you are in a position to help others.'

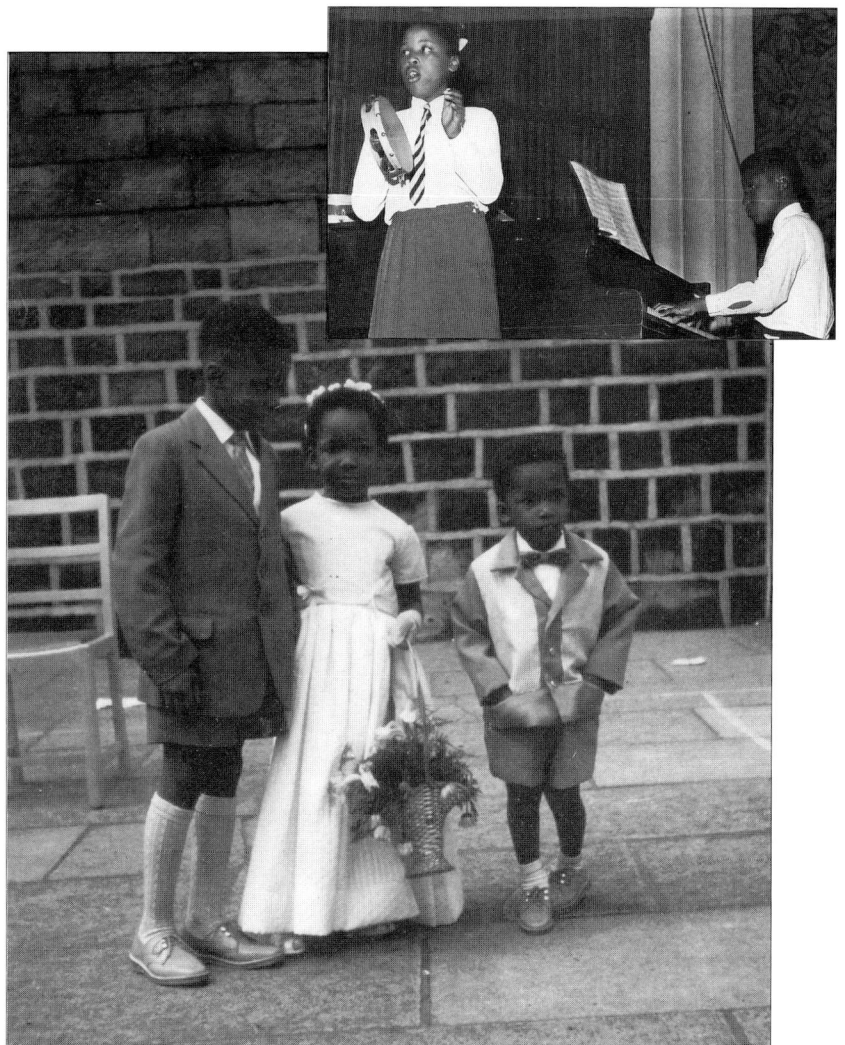

Trevor, Judy and David Padmore. 1962 school yard – Lord Street Whit Walks. Inset: Melanie and Wayne Marshall in concert.

Ivan, Elaine and Judy Padmore on left of photograph c1960 with friends at a wedding

Costella Marshall with Wayne William, 1961

'I never got any job from the Labour Exchange. I kept calling at every place I passed asking for work. I went to Ferrantis once. When the man saw me, he said, "You've come to the wrong place!" and never told me where he thought the right place was... "Have you had any experience?" Well of course you haven't, they knew you had only just arrived. Then years later, the climate had changed somewhat and I got a job at Ferrantis – still with no experience – because by that time people had got used to seeing a few coloured faces.'

'I went to the Cairo Mill in Waterhead – they told me right away – "No jobs!" But he did say to me "They are taking some of your lads on the buses", however I went and started on the buses. I knew I must break away somehow, so in 1960, I started going to night school for G.C.E. subjects at the School of Commerce where the headmaster was Mr. Lamb. I got some qualifications, including an O.N.C. in business studies. It was then that I went back to Ferrantis and was taken on without question. It was nights, which meant I had to leave my wife alone with five children. On my time off, I would go round lots of firms, taking all my certificates, which I was convinced by now would be all I needed. My English was excellent, I had spoken it from birth. I decided at this time that it was possibly my colour .... and then .... in 1966 for the first time ever,

the trees began to part and I caught a glimpse of the road ahead. The Personnel Officer of one firm said to me "Why are you applying for these menial jobs with your qualifications?" He said, "We have other vacancies here on the office side. If you want to give it a go, I will have a word with the Departmental Head". At first, he didn't welcome me at all, he made no secret of it, stating that he was worried how the girls might react. The Personnel Officer stuck to his principles and appointed me.'

Vishnu Mohandas was born in Mombasa, Kenya in 1935. He worked on the railway and enjoyed his job – it was a clerical position and his English was excellent. In 1956 he got married and although the marriage was arranged, Vishnu still had a say in the matter.

'My father went first to different families and selected three or four girls who he thought would be suitable and compatible. He saw the parents of course and during this time it was usual to make lots of enquiries – re family and health and educational standards and if the chosen girl would be a good wife and mother and be agreeable to the match. I saw a couple of the girls and didn't like them, so when I chose my wife, although it is somewhat arranged, it is agreeable.'

In 1964 Kenya became independent and the Mohandas family, like many others at that time, were British.

'We were given the choice of becoming a citizen of Kenya and forgoing our British nationality and were told that jobs would be given first to Kenyans. We all felt reluctant to take what we thought was a drastic step and we decided to go to India in 1965 where our roots and our relatives were.'

'In 1967 I came to Oldham and lodged first in Moss-Side. Because I had always done clerical work I went to the railway for work and was offered work as a guard. I remember mostly when I came, it seemed very cold and dark – it was October. The people who saw me for interview would not accept that I could do office work.'

Vishnu's wife used to cry, they had many regrets coming to England and felt that it was some sort of punishment. Life in Mombasa had been pleasant, hours on the railway were easy to manage, with 12.30pm-2pm at lunchtime when the sun was high in the sky and every five years – 4 months paid holiday.

'I got a job at the Chadderton Mill eventually. It was a non-union firm, at the time I didn't quite understand the implication. I signed a contract to work 60 hours a week, which I was glad to do, because I was being paid £22.10sh.

There were girls training us, German, Spanish, Polish and Italian and honestly my English was much better than theirs. I was sending £50 a month home to my family through the District Bank, because I am the eldest and this is the way we do.'

'I got a room in Werneth with an Indian couple for £2.50 per week. It was very good and we managed until I saved for a deposit for a house and in 1968, only one year after I came I got a house and it was £650.'

'One day in the mill the foreman looked down the passageway where we worked and whistled to me. The girls said, "he wants you – you had better go." He whistled again and I didn't go, I said "I'm not going, I'm not a dog!" The girls looked very disturbed and shocked, but he came down to me and called me to one side and apologised. He knew I worked hard and he said because it was so noisy in the mill, he was used to doing that. We got on with each other after that episode and one day he said to me "Can you do up to 8 pm?" So I did from 6am to 8pm and then a couple of weeks later he said "Can you do up to 10pm?" I know it was exploitation, but I did it because I wanted to save up. Then one day I saw a job advertised for a hospital porter at Boundary Park. There were nine of us applied, I was the only coloured person and I got it. I felt it was a real achievement.'

Below: View from kitchen of our first house

First coach trip to Blackpool organised by the Indian Association Oldham in 1969.

Belle Vue 1969, the Mohandas family.

'I came to England in 1962 and to Oldham in December 1963. I had friends here so I came to them. I was passing the Sun Mill on Peel Street, the day I came. I saw the gaffer and asked him if he had any vacancies. He said I could start so I was very pleased. The firm operated knitting machines and I was a trainee for two weeks. In 1964 I bought my first house with my brother who had come over to England also. In 1966 I went to Bangladesh to find a wife. My situation was slightly different than usual because my father had died – so I had no chance to talk about it. He would have played an active part in choosing a wife for me. I had a female cousin, who I was very close to and when I had chosen the person I wanted to marry I asked my cousin to speak to the mother of the girl! I sent money home through the post office – I had sisters and I was the eldest son.'

When Jagdish Kumar Sisodia arrived in England in 1963, there were very few Indian people living in Oldham at that time. He formed a joint Indian Association in 1964 with Ashton and Stalybridge and he was elected President. Mr Sisodia had obtained his Bachelor of Law degree at Bombay University and became a judge in his own country. He was the strongest link with the town's Indian community, encouraging them in every way possible. Unfortunately Mr Sisodia died suddenly in 1968 at a crucial time as the immigration population increased tremendously during 1967 and 1968.

The majority of Indians who have settled in Oldham are Gujuratis, some from the Gujarat State of India and others from Africa. Other Indians come from Punjab, Maharashtra and Madras.

'My father came to Oldham first in 1963. He was a Judge in India – in Gujurat. He had been on a tour – he had friends in Africa – in Kenya and England was the last stop. I think he must have had a reason, because he was worried about his children's future. At that time, India was very unstable. However, I believe he wrote to us and suggested we came, my Mother immediately said, "No!". By 1965 however we were here. We came by coach overnight – Yelloway. It was raining, dark and cold in the early morning. Nobody to be seen, my father eventually got a taxi and took us to the house he had purchased on Slater Street. It seemed to my mother and my brothers and sisters that it was much worse than we had left behind us, we had left sunshine and a very decent home.

The people on Slater Street were absolutely marvellous. Nobody could have had a better welcome, everyone – all the neighbours tried to help us with the language – with everything. Within a few days, we could see the good side and felt the warmth of the Oldham people.'

'An association was soon formed and my father became the President. We had a lot of organised activities after this.'

'At St. Thomas's School there were only two immigrant boys – then in September I went to Hollins school. In the geography lesson I saw "Bombay" and told the boy next to me, that was where I came from. "Miss", he said, "Bharat comes from Bombay". The teacher, Mrs Kempe was wonderful. She got the whole map of India and put it on the classroom wall. The tremendous care she took with her teaching and making me welcome was very good.'

Indian Festival Oldham 1968. This took place at King Street Co-op Hall.

When I die, then make my grave
High on an ancient mound
In my own beloved Ukraine
In steppeland without bound:
Whence one may see wide-skirted wheatlands
Dnipro's steep-cliffed shore,
There whence one may hear the blustering
River wildly roar.

In the aftermath of the second world war, there were over a million displaced persons of varying nationalities in Europe who, for one reason or another, could not return to their homelands. Many thousands of these were Ukrainians who had served in the war as forced labourers in Germany. Both Ukrainian displaced persons and prisoners of war were ultimately offered refuge in the West as E.V.W.'s (European Volunteer Workers) and approximately 30,000 came to Britain.

Speaking on behalf of the Ministry of Labour in 1949, Sir Godfrey Ince said the acceptance of refugees was "partly an act of charity and partly to suit ourselves" – this last bit refers to the placing of displaced persons, (D.P.'s as they became known) in under-manned, usually low-paid, industries to make good, Britain's labour shortage.

'We came to a hostel. There was already a few Polish girls living there. We had bed and breakfast. Then a lady came from the Fox Mill, Hollinwood. The factory, at first you are frightened of touching anything – but it was surprising how quickly we learned. We got three guineas and had to pay 30 shillings for our lodgings and had the rest to live on and buy our meals. The people at work, they helped us and would explain. I never felt a foreigner in this country!'

World War 2 uprooted millions of Ukrainians from their ancestral lands, and some of them were given the chance to settle in Oldham. They had few material possessions, but they brought with them what they treasured most, their Christian faith, their traditions and their thousand year old culture. They settled into the local community and now play a part in cultural and political life.

Right: Madelaine Yaworsky and her landlady in Oldham Park c1947.

Below: Yaworsky children in the centre with friends.

'I came to England because it was the nearest to home – it was never our intention to stay – we always wanted to eventually go home. That feeling never leaves you.'

'The landlady didn't know our needs. It was the language of course. It was very hard because we couldn't communicate – but we were going forward. We started finding our own people, we found we could write letters to friends we had been with in Germany. We had to organise ourselves, we didn't have to run any more, we had a sort of freedom. When I saw a policeman though, I felt afraid for a long time.'

The refugees came to Britain after years of hardship and danger and the majority were unable to speak any English. Given this background, they adjusted well to life in Oldham, starting up their own Church, forming a community with the local people and contributing to Oldham's economic growth.

'The worst thing was when we had our children – we had nobody to help us – our children had no grandparents – the children would ask when they came home from school, "where are *my* Grandma and Grandpa?"'

Madelaine and friend, Oldham park, 1947.

Erika Forstna and Oleksander Korolczuk 30th May 1953. Married at the Ukraine Orthodox Church, Onchan Avenue. The Church was purchased by the Ukraines in 1952.

Above top: Whit-walks. Ukrainian children c 1962 – Nadia Kwas – holding ribbons.

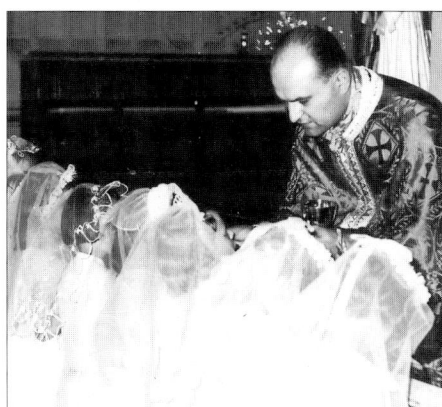

Above: 1st Holy Communion at St. Patrick's, The Ukraine community would hire the Church for the day prior to acquiring their own church.

Right: Nadia Kwas

Above: Olga and Harry Butterworth married at Hanover, Germany. 'There were no clothes to buy, very few items at all. A friend lent me the dress.

Below:Whit-Friday, Union Street, 1950's. Temperance Billiard Hall and Union Street, Methodist Church in background.

'After the uprising in 1944 I was taken from Warsaw to Magdeburg by the Germans. The uprising had lasted two months and during this time we were without food or water and many, many people died. They took us in cattle trucks – to a place about 7 kilometres away where we were segregated and split from our parents. My father was in the Middle East, so my mother had to take my two little sisters to the south of Poland where she had relatives who could provide them with one room. I didn't see my mother or sisters again for thirteen years.

The young people like my other sister and myself were sent to forced labour camps and one thing we had to do was work in the sugar beet fields. Thinking about it now, I suppose it was funny actually, but we couldn't do it – we were city girls, so when they realised this, we were put to work in the sugar beet factory.

We stayed there until the war finished – the Americans came and told us there would be no transport available for 12 months. By this time, the Americans and the English were pulling out and Magdeburg was given to the Russians.'

'Harry's regiment transported us all to Hanover, Germany. After a lot of difficulty we got married in Hanover and the Army gave us a wonderful wedding.'

'Ten years ago, I could not have spoken of my separation from my parents, it still distressed me after all the years. I tried many times to visit Poland, but was refused and then in 1956 I was permitted to go. Everything was arranged and my visa didn't arrive. I wanted to give up, but Harry said "No, you must go now, you have looked forward to it for so long" so we went to London to the Polish Embassy and the Russian Embassy and that way I got a visa, and flew a day later than planned.'

Polish people began to put down roots and set up new communities, although they never gave up hope of someday returning to a free Poland. It was felt by all Polish people that it was very important to honour the Polish customs and traditions, at the same time respecting the ways and traditions of the people who had welcomed them into their lives and communities, thus enriching both.

The end of the war had found many Poles far from everything that was familiar to them. Although Britain offered a place to the Polish refugees, it was accepted with a sad reluctance because the country they had struggled and fought for was not free.

Left: Whit-walks, Oldham town centre c1960's.

Below: A Polish Bishop visiting Oldham.

'When I came to Oldham in 1950, I felt a warm welcome immediately and here – in Oldham, so many of us had come from camps or orphanages. I myself was in an orphanage, because my parents had died in Russia. I learned to speak some English at this time, but many of the conditions that Polish people had to endure in these camps with their crowded conditions made Oldham seem to me a place where I felt I could breathe for the first time, and some of us were very lucky that we could communicate.'

'Some Polish people were already in Oldham, they had arrived in 1947 chiefly for industry and many were employed by the Corporation on transport. My husband had graduated from the Polish School of Medicine in Edinburgh after the war and came to Oldham as a G.P.'

'In 1963 I started to hold the Guide meetings at my house on Sunday morning after Mass at St. Patrick's. At that time I was everything in the company – leader, treasurer and contact between other Guide companies. The Guide movement is a wonderful idea, because it crosses all barriers, the girls used to have a lovely time discussing different ideas and contributing towards projects.'

'In 1969, on the 25th Anniversary of the liberation of Monte Cassino, in Italy, twelve Polish Guides went from Oldham to participate in the event. It was a wonderful experience for them and taught them a lot about the background of Poland and the sentiments of the Polish people.'

You are now an elderly woman of great beauty,
strong and serene,
At home with the elements, and as it were,
used to taming foreigners, birds and squirrels,
And although – unawares – your face drifts off
into layers of sadness.
This has only been known to happen when
gates are closed after children,
Or when – in between courses – a door bangs
in the draught, and all of a sudden
There is nothing whatever to say.

Zofia Ilinska.

Polish Guides displaying the rug lovingly knitted for Oxfam 1967.

'The Chronicle covered all the events and happenings while the twin town people were in Oldham and that is how I met Martin. We married the following year at Coldhurst Parish Church.'

'I was President of the Youth Organisation in my home town, which was Kranj. I was a textile chemist with a minute knowledge of English. When we came to Oldham in July 1967 as a group, because Oldham was the twin town of Kranj, we stayed at Castleshaw camp school. It seemed cut off from everywhere, but we weren't allowed to go out anyway. I remember writing to my mother and telling her that I was still reading without a lamp and it was 10pm. I was amazed that it was still light in the evening, at home it went dark so early.'

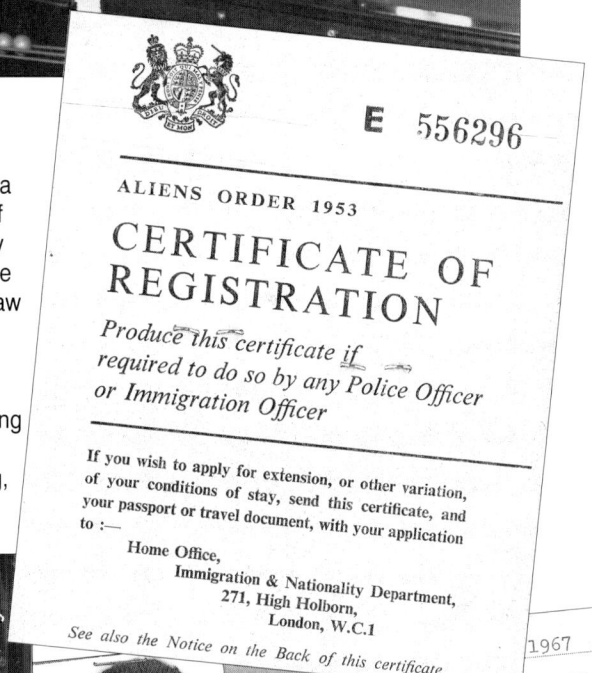

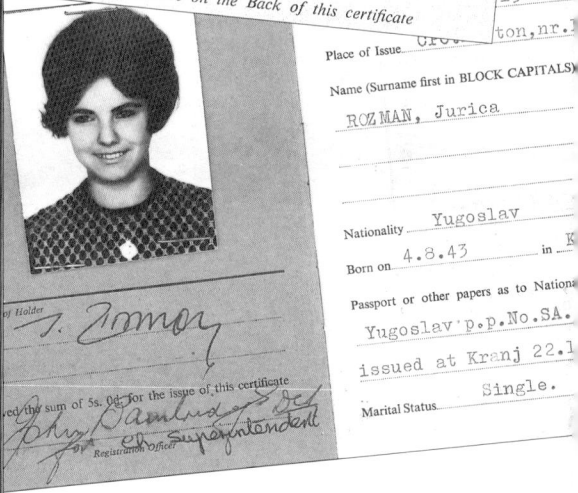

E 556296

ALIENS ORDER 1953

CERTIFICATE OF REGISTRATION

Produce this certificate if required to do so by any Police Officer or Immigration Officer

If you wish to apply for extension, or other variation, of your conditions of stay, send this certificate, and your passport or travel document, with your application to :—

Home Office,
Immigration & Nationality Department,
271, High Holborn,
London, W.C.1

See also the Notice on the Back of this certificate

1967

Place of Issue... ...ton, nr.

Name (Surname first in BLOCK CAPITALS)

ROZMAN, Jurica

Nationality ... Yugoslav

Born on 4.8.43 ... in K

Passport or other papers as to Nationa

Yugoslav P.P.No.SA.

issued at Kranj 22.1

Marital Status ... Single.

Above: Jurica's Certificate of registration.

Left: Jurica Rozman married to Martin Smith, Coldhurst Church 1967.

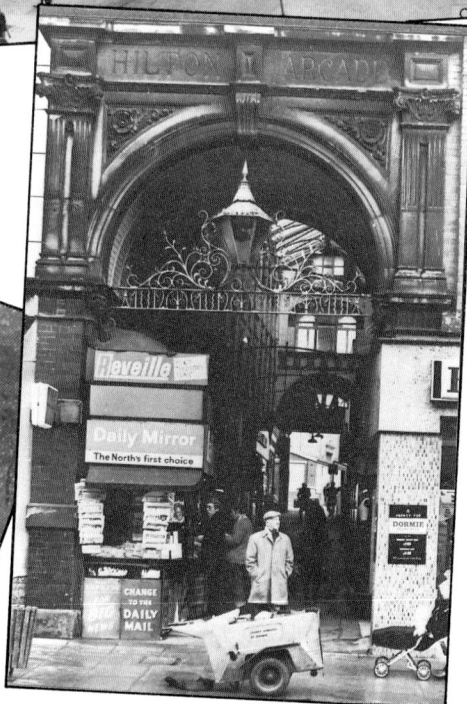

Photographs, from top to bottom:
Music time, Springhead School c1949
Looking towards Mumps, 1950's
Weighing and Measuring, Werneth School c1956
Hilton Arcade 1960's
Butler Green Mission Scouts at Hardcastle Crags 1920's